PEERAGE BOOKS

EUROPEAN
GLASS

European
Glass

TEXT BY OLGA DRAHOTOVÁ
PHOTOGRAPHS BY GABRIEL URBÁNEK
DRAWINGS BY IVAN KAFKA

Contents

Published in Great Britain 1983
by Peerage Books
59 Grosvenor Street, London
W1

© Artia, Prague 1983

ISBN 0 907408 75 3

Printed in Czechoslovakia
2/09/04/51-01

Designed and produced by Artia
Text by Olga Drahotová
Translated by Norah Hronková
Photographs by Gabriel Urbánek
(All depicted objects come from the
collection of the Museum of Decorative Arts
in Prague, except illustrations no. 140 —
Museum of Glass in Kamenický Šenov, and
no. 145 — Museum of Glass and Jewellery in
Jablonec nad Nisou)
Drawings by Ivan Kafka
Graphic design by Pavel Hrach

The Craft of Glassmaking

In every work of art beauty and style are closely linked with the artist's mastery of the technique of production and understanding of the laws governing the given material. To appreciate them every glass collector should know the basic facts about glass production.

Glass is made of sand melted in a glass furnace with the aid of alkaline fluxing agents, i. e. substances that facilitate the melting of the sand. Chemically glass is a silicate. Its main components are silicon dioxide (70—75 %) and alkaline oxides — soda or potash. Another important component of glass is calcium oxide, which stabilizes it. From the physical aspect glass is a liquid in a solid state. As a liquid it has a tendency in some circumstances to crystalize. The properties of glass change according to its composition. Soda glass is soft and malleable, it hardens relatively slowly and so it can be made into complicated shapes over a long time. All ancient glass was soda glass, as was Venetian glass and glass à la façon de Venise from the 15th to the 18th centuries. The soda was obtained from the ash of seaweed by leaching, the potash from the ash of deciduous trees. In contrast to the soda, the potash had to go through a complicated process of cleaning, so that the glass should not be coloured or sullied. North of the Alps it has been used as a fluxing agent since the 11th century. Potash glass is hard and hardens quickly. At first a greenish Waldglas was made of it, then — after the techniques of cleaning and decolourizing had been mastered — also crystal glass, which was very suitable for cutting and engraving. When lead oxide (Pb_2O_3) is used as a fluxing agent what is called lead crystal is formed — an easily melted, relatively soft glass with a high shine and a high refractive index, such as has been made in England since the 17th century. In the last quarter of the 18th century it was discovered to be the most suitable glass for complicated cutting.

The natural colour of glass is green-ish or brownish, according to various undesirable admixtures (in the first place compounds of iron). Clear glass can only be obtained by cleaning the raw materials and decolourizing the glass. This decolourizing is done on either a physical or a chemical basis. In the first method the principle of complementary colours is used, the green colour being covered by its complementary colour, reddish violet: most frequently manganese dioxide (MnO_2) has been used for this. In the chemical method oxidizing substances are added to the glass batch, for instance arsenic (As_2O_3) or saltpetre (KNO_3). This oxidizes the iron contained in the raw materials — trivalent iron then colours the glass fifteen times less strongly than bivalent iron.

Oxides of metal colour the glass in many different ways: iron, according to its valence, makes it green, blue or yellow, copper makes it blue, green or red, cobalt blue, gold ruby red, nickel and manganese violet, chromium and uranium green, cadmium and sulphur yellow. In modern times selenium, cerium, praseodymium and neodymium are also used for colouring glass.

In the earliest days glass used to be melted in open pot furnaces, but gradually the melting technique was perfected and in Roman times excellent types of furnace were already known. In olden times the glass was shaped by winding it on a pottery core, by making it of slices of coloured canes (mosaic glass and millefiori), by melting cullet in two-piece moulds or by the lost-wax process (cire perdue). Since the beginning of the Christian period glass has most often been formed by blowing.

The first person to work at the glass furnace is the teaser, who sees to the composition of the glass batch and the correct viscosity of the molten glass. The glass-blower or his mate then takes up the honey-thick gather on a hollow blow-pipe and, by alternately blowing and rolling on a marble table (marvering), forms it into a bubble. This is constantly reheated, so that it remains pliable, further molten glass is gathered on it and it is shaped with various instruments in a mould; it is then the basis for every blown product. Layers of different coloured glass may be added to the paraison, it can be turned into a window roundel or blown into two-piece wooden moulds, which determine its shape. What is called optical decoration is made by blowing the paraison into ribbed or other moulds bearing the relief decoration, then with further blowing the relief loses its plasticity and is visible only optically. At the furnace glass is also decorated by threading (laying on drawn-out threads), pincering, combing, etc. Then too coloured glass blobs can be embedded in the hot paraison. Mosaic glass and millefiori are made by melting slices of coloured canes into the paraison, which is thus covered with bright, repeated patterns. To make trailed or network glass the gather is blown into a smooth metal mould, in which different-coloured canes are prepared and these then form filigree ornaments on it. The Venetians developed the various techniques of glass production and decoration most perfectly, as their soft slow-hardening glass allowed great virtuosity in shaping while hot. Glass may also be iridized in the glass furnace, i. e. coloured in rainbow hues by means of metal salts. The glass when ready must cool slowly in a cooling furnace.

The cooled product can then be further decorated by engraving with a diamond point, or wheel-engraved or cut — either in intaglio or in relief. Since the 16th century an engraving machine has been used for this, worked by a treadle, and then a similar cutting lathe. For relief cutting, in which the background of the ornament is ground away, water power was used. Grinding is done either by a rotating horizontal grinding disc (faceting, grinding the bottom and edges), or by vertical wheels of varying profiles. The grinding powder is fine sand mixed with water. In this way rounded, v-shaped, flat or other cuts are ground.

Engraving is done with smaller rotating wheels, mostly of copper, the spindle of which is fixed to the shaft of the engraving machine. The wheels and heads are of different sizes and profiles, and the engraver changes them according to need. Their edges are smeared with emery powder mixed with oil; this mixture then engraves decoration into the glass according to a drawn model. Wheels of lead and poplar wood are used for polishing.

Painting on glass is either fired (painting with enamels) or unfired (paintings with oil and varnish paints). Enamels are vitreous colours — either opaque or transparent. They are coloured with the oxides of metal and contain a good deal of lead, so as to be easily meltable. They only get their brilliant colours once they are fired in a muffle furnace. Glass is also painted with gold, silver and lustres, which are metal oxides dissolved in acid and mixed with an oil or varnish medium. In addition there exist two stains, yellow and red, which are colours from silver or copper salts, mixed with what is known as yellow clay: these are also fired in a muffle furnace. In the Bor region black staining has also been used since 1914. (This "staining" should not be confused with "stained glass", in which mostly ordinary coloured glass was used.)

Etching on glass was done by Heinrich Schwanhardt in Nuremberg as early as the second half of the 17th century. But it is still not clear what acid he used, as the only effective one seems to be hydrofluoric acid, which was not discovered until 1777.

Besides blowing, hollow glass can also be shaped by pressing and blowing at-the-lamp. Glass pressing, introduced in the USA in 1827, is a semi-automatic process, during which the glass attains its form and decoration at the same time, with the use of three-piece moulds and plungers. The glass is shaped over an oil lamp (or later a gas one) from prefabricated pipes and canes, which are re-heated. This technique was first used in Venice in the making of beads; later little figures were shaped at-the-lamp and, since the 19th century, vessels as well.

Advice to Collectors and Recommended Literature

R. Schmidt's book *Das Glas,* Berlin 1912, 2nd edition, 1922, is still the basic handbook for historians and collectors, although its information has been greatly added to and made more exact. After the Second World War a number of books were published, of which the best are: W. Honey, *Glass,* Victoria and Albert Museum, London 1946, and E. Barrington-Haynes, *Glass Through the Ages,* London 1959. Most of the post-war collected German works are based on the book by R. Schmidt: W. Bernt, *Altes Glas,* Munich 1950, J. Jantzen, *Deutsches Glas aus fünf Jahrhunderten,* Düsseldorf 1960, I. Schlosser, *Das alte Glas,* Brunswick 1956, new edition 1965, F. Kämpfer, *Viertausend Jahre Glas,* Dresden 1965, and others. Newer information is contained in G. Weiss, *Ullstein-Gläserbuch,* Berlin-Frankfurt-Wien 1966. A very reliable book was published in Holland, H. E. van Gelder, *Glas en Ceramiek,* Utrecht 1955. A modern view is given by A. Polak, *Glass, Its Makers and Its Public,* London 1975, which treats the subject sociologically. Of still later works there is an invaluable handbook by H. Newman, *An Illustrated Dictionary of Glass,* London 1977, which is a very carefully compiled dictionary on the history and technology of glass. An older dictionary by E. M. Elville, *The Collector's Dictionary of Glass,* London 1961, mainly concerns English glass. For the history of technology the most extensive aid are the chapters on the history of glass technology in the five-volume work by Singer et al., *A History of Technology,* vols. 1—5, Oxford 1954—8, while briefer information on the same subject is given by W. Schnauck, *Glaslexikon,* Munich 1959. Some help with individual points is given in the specialized catalogues of public and private collections given in the bibliography. Scientific information in a very readable literary form comes in the latest publication of the Corning Museum by R. J. Charleston, *Masterpieces of Glass. A World History from the Corning Museum of Glass,* New York 1980. For information on the prices of glass there is a useful survey published by W. Spiegl, "Glas", *Battenberg Antiquitäten Kataloge,* Munich 1979.

The Roots of European Glassmaking
Ancient Glass and Early Medieval Glass

No exact date can be given for the invention of glass. It originated gradually in the Bronze Age during the years 5000 and 4000 B.C. as a by-product of ceramics production; certainly experience in metal and stoneworking was used too. The direct predecessor of glass were vitreous glazes covering ceramic jewels, wall friezes and pots. Latest research shows that glass was first made in western Asia, not in Egypt. The first glass objects to be made were opaque beads of various colours. Discoveries of such beads in Syria go back to 5000 B.C., whereas in Egypt their occurrence has only been proved around the middle of 4000 B.C. The oldest known fragments of hollow pots are also of Near Eastern origin: they come from Mesopotamia from the end of the 16th century B.C.

At this time the only things to be made of glass were small objects, jewels, pendants and amulets, then containers such as vials for scented oils and cosmetics, small cups and bowls. Almost all vessels were shaped using the technique of a sandy core, somewhere around 10 cm in size. This technique of shaping glass on a sandy core was slow and laborious. The glassblower placed a core of the required shape on a metal rod (the core was not only of sand, but a mixture of sand, clay and straw). He then either dipped this in the liquid glass or wound hot glass threads around it. By further heating and rolling on a smooth stone

table (marvering) the surface of the vessel was smoothed and finally the core was scraped out. The glass was melted in primitive pot furnaces, which have been directly proved in the archaeological finds at Tell-el-Amarna from the 14th century B.C. The melting process was done in two phases. First the glass batch was made in clay pots at a low temperature (pre-fritted). After cooling the upper and lower impure layers were broken off, the remainder crushed and melted again at a temperature of about 1100°C.

Ancient glass was always soda glass with a high alkali content, which made it possible to melt it at low temperatures and at the same time gave the substance longer malleability. Colourfulness is typical of pre-Roman glass, as it was used as a substitute for precious and semi-precious stones. The earliest glass was almost always opaque, most often dark blue, less frequently turquoise blue, black or green. The decoration of the vessels consisted of applied threads of yellow, white, turquoise and green, combed into garland or zigzag motifs and rolled into the surface of the vessel.

The beginnings of the production of hollow glass in Egypt are proved by three vessels bearing the name of Pharaoh Thutmosis III (1504—1430 B.C.), now in museums in London, Munich and New York. Researchers consider that the development of glassmaking in Egypt is connected with the Near

Little mug of light blue glass with the emblem of Thutmosis III (1504—1450 B.C.), shaped on a sandy core. One of the first glass vessels, Egypt, around 1500 B.C.

Glass, 1st half of 1st century (1—8)

Pyxis, made by melting various coloured canes, some of which contained powdered gold leaf, Roman, perhaps from Alexandria between 50 B.C. and 25 A.D.

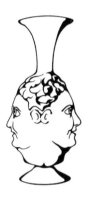

Little bottle, blown into a three-piece mould, the body in the form of a head with two faces, called a Janus bottle, Roman, 1st—2nd century A.D.

Eastern campaigns by this Pharaoh, which probably brought Near Eastern glassmakers to Egypt amongst the numerous prisoners. From the 15th century glassmaking in Egypt and Mesopotamia developed in parallel for three centuries and spread from there to Cyprus and the Aegean. The 18th dynasty — Thutmosis III, Amenhotep III and IV — was one of the greatest development of Egyptian glassmaking. The shapes of the vessels were taken from examples made from other materials, ceramics, metal and stone. The most beautiful objects have been preserved from the time of the rule of Amenhotep IV — Akhenaten, a heretical Pharaoh from 1370 to 1358 B.C., whose seat was in Tell-el-Amarna. At the end of the Bronze Age (after 1200), when the Egyptian New Empire was going through a period of anarchy and gradual dissolution, the production of vessels ceased altogether, and only beads, seals and amulets continued to be made. Then Egypt retired into the background for many centuries, and glassmaking only came to life there again in the Hellenic Period.

On the other hand, in the Near East there was a new renaissance of glassmaking from the 9th century B.C.; the main centres were Syria and Mesopotamia, and the enterprising Phoenicians organized extensive trade in glass throughout the Mediterranean area. In the 7th and 6th centuries the making of glass on a sandy core was revived, similar to the older Egyptian method from the 14th and 13th centuries, first in Mesopotamia, later on the eastern coast of the Mediterranean, on the shores of the Black Sea and also in the Aegean area, in Rhodes and Cyprus.

These later vials for scented oils, called balsamaria, mostly follow the contemporary Greek ceramics: the amphoriskos, aryballos, oenochoë. The conical alabastron was modelled on older alabaster vessels. At this time the most important technical inspiration evidently came from Mesopotamia. Under Sargon II (722—705) there were glassworks and workshops in Nimrud and Nineveh. The first recipes for making glass come from the 7th century, and they have been preserved on hieroglyphic tablets. Besides the technique of wrapping glass on a core, another method started to be used at that time: cutting vessels from a block of glass, and also the mosaic technique, in which slices cut from glass rods of different colours were placed in a mould and fused by slow melting. Another new technique was melting crushed frits in two-piece moulds and the cire perdue method, when molten glass poured into moulds of clay and plaster took on the shape of the wax original. But the greatest legacy of Mesopotamian glassmaking, apart from the mosaic technique, was the artistic use and perfection of the technique of grinding. Shallow bowls of almost colourless glass date from the 7th to the 5th centuries, which were melted in two-piece moulds and decorated with deeply cut radial grooves or leaf rosettes. The production of these bowls was continued even when the Persians ruled Babylon in the 5th and 4th centuries, during the reign of the Achaemenid dynasty. In the meantime glassmaking had spread further to Greece, to Crete and perhaps even to Italy.

After the year 330 there were great changes in the political and cultural

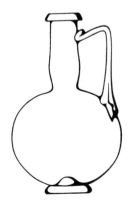

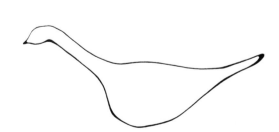

Covered urn,
Roman, 1st century A.D.

Four-sided mould-blown
bottle. A common ancient
container,
Syria, 1st—4th century A.D.

picture of the civilized world of those days: the campaigns of Alexander the Great brought an expansion of Greek culture in the Near East. Mesopotamia, then pushed to the margin of cultural events, stopped glass production too, whereas the glasshouses in Syria prospered, though they only produced relatively simple goods, such as for instance palm cups melted in moulds and finished by grinding. Lower Egypt, with the newly founded Alexandria, became the most important centre of Greek culture in the Near East. Undoubtedly, Mesopotamian glassmakers and cutters gathered there too, and so the production of mosaic glass, glass melted in two-piece moulds and lost wax continued there as well. All these techniques were further developed and perfected in the Near East, as was the cutting and wheel-engraving. Luxury glass was exported from Alexandria to Italy, Greece and elsewhere. Enamel painting on glass was developed there too, and the entirely new technique of decorating glass with engraved gold leaf between two layers of glass, an example of which is the well-known bowl from Canosa, now in London. Some of the Alexandrian craftsmen moved to follow their rich customers and much of the typically Alexandrian work was in fact made in Italy.

Just before the Christian period there came a great turning-point in glassmaking, indeed a revolution. The glassmakers' blowpipe was invented, which made the production of blown glass possible and became the glassmakers' basic instrument, unchanged until today, directly determining the character of glass for a further two thousand years. This revolutionary invention, thanks to which the use of glass became general, was essentially a very simple step. In making glass on a clay core the hot glass liquid was picked up on a metal rod: in the Bronze Age on a bronze one, but in the first millennium B.C. on an iron one. Someone had the idea of replacing the solid rod with a hollow one, through which it was possible to blow the glass into thin bubbles. This invention, evidently rightly ascribed to the Phoenicians, meant that the production of glass was many times speeded up, simplified and cheapened.

At first the older techniques of shaping were used in parallel with that of blowing. The mosaic technique and melting of glass in moulds remained exclusively for luxury glass, while blown glass was mostly functional. But by the second half of the first century A. D. blown glass already outweighed glass melted in moulds. The first blown products we know include various unguentaria — spherical, bulbous and drawn out — hemispherical palm cups and bowls, domed and four-sided bottles and ewers. Some types of glass were blown to their final shape in multi-piece relief moulds as bottles in the shape of grapes, shells, dates, human heads etc., or as cups with almond-shaped nodules or low relief figured decoration.

During the first century Syrian-type glass gradually spread over the whole of the Roman Empire, as Syrian glassmakers not only exported glass, but themselves founded glassworks outside Syria, first in the Aegean area and later in what correspond to today's Italy, France and the Rhineland. In the 2nd and 3rd centuries they penetrated

Glass, 2nd half of 1st century
(1—5)

Goblet with pincered decoration of twisted trails and shells, Rhineland, 4th century

Beaker decorated with applied sinuous threads, Rhineland, 2nd and 3rd centuries

still further — to the territory of present-day Spain, Belgium, Holland, Switzerland and Britain. This is how it happened that glassmaking developed quite uniformly in the first three centuries A.D. in the eastern and western parts of the Mediterranean area, and only a few types of glass can be called typical of a certain region. In those days contacts between the east and west of the empire were constant and lively. It is hard to judge now whether this was due to the increase of trade or to the establishment of the eastern glassmakers in the west.

Archaeological finds in Italy, Belgium, Holland, Germany, Britain and elsewhere include a relatively large quantity of containers, besides glass for the household: bottles for cosmetics and perfumes, and also bigger vessels for wine and oil. Some of the bottles have a name stamped in the bottom, such as Ennion of Sidon, Sentia Secunda of Aquileia, or Frontinus, who appears to have worked in Gaul. In most cases, however, we do not know whether the name indicates the glassmaker, the owner of the glasshouse, or the producer of the contents of the bottle.

In the east Alexandria remained the most important centre. Even in Roman times the production of luxury glass continued here, probably mainly for export. The famous Portland Vase of dark blue white-layered glass with relief cut figured decoration originated some time at the beginning of the Christian period. It is, undoubtedly, like other similar work, from the hands of Alexandrian artists, whether working in Egypt or Italy.

Since the end of the 2nd century in Alexandria clear glass was replacing the older mosaic and coloured layered glass. Cutting and engraving are used on this perfectly clear glass in a different way which suits the translucent material. Clear glass predominated in the production of luxury glass in general at the end of the 2nd century. This can be seen from vessels decorated with sinuous applied threads coiled round them. At that time they were probably made in Syria and in Cyprus, afterwards they were brought to the west, where they caught on mainly in the Rhineland in the 2nd and 3rd centuries. A further example of the spread of eastern techniques to the western part of the Roman Empire are the fondi d'oro, as they are called — double-walled medallions set into the bottoms of cups etc., decorated with engraving in gold leaf: the preserved pieces are mostly fragments of bowls found in the Roman catacombs from the 3rd and 4th centuries. They are undoubtedly taken from old Alexandrian models from the 3rd century B.C.

The constant contacts between the east and west of the Roman Empire suddenly ceased in the 4th century when Constantinople was promoted to a capital and the old single empire was divided into the Eastern and Western Roman Empires. The migration of glassmakers stopped and production in the east and west began to differ, especially in the shapes that originated in the 4th century. In the west the Rhineland production in Cologne dominated, artistically developing types of decoration known from the east: threading mainly making use of the contrast between the clear glass vessels and coloured threads, linear cutting or em-

Glass, 2nd century (1—6)

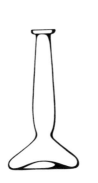

[15

Beaker with cut openwork outer net, called vas diatretum, Rome or Rhineland, 4th century

Bottle with engraved view of Baiae, Roman, probably Puteoli, end of 3rd or 4th century

bedded blobs — of different coloured glass. Even though, with the gradual decline of the Roman Empire, the standard of glassmaking also declined in ordinary production, excellent and unique luxury objects were still being made in the 4th century, such as the vasa diatreta, cups wrapped in an outer net, only loosely joined to the inner casing, with an inscription or even figured decoration; these can be seen in museums in Cologne, Vienna, Milan and London. Experts still dispute the technique used to make them. The majority of researchers are convinced that they were melted in the mould and that the outer free plastic decoration was made by grinding and cutting with incredible mastery. It is thought that these cups, decorated with a network attached by struts, could have been made in the Rhineland but that there existed at the same time other productions of this type of glass, such as for instance the Lycurgus cup in the British Museum in London or the Situla Pagana in the treasury of St. Mark's Cathedral in Venice, which are considered to be of Italian make.

The products of the provincial glassworks, though made in many places in the western Roman Empire in the 4th century, were neither numerous nor of high quality. In the 4th century and more particularly in the 5th, many changes were evident in the whole of the west Roman and in the Cologne production, due to the general decline of Roman culture. The shape and decoration of the glass were more and more influenced by the taste of the Teuton customers, and so the name Frankish glass is used for this post-Roman glass. The number of shapes was

reduced and the decorative techniques restricted to trailed elements and optical decoration from moulds, sometimes the embedding of white threads. The glass is impure, it ceased to be purified, and so it is more or less bottle green in colour. Drinking horns were made, footed beakers, cone-shaped beakers, bell-shaped and shallow bowls. In the 6th century hemispherical palm cups appeared. Modelled on the late Rhineland beakers with applied fish and shells are the claw beakers (Rüsselbecher), which are decorative rather than functional, and occur in finds of the 5th — 8th centuries in Germany and also in Britain and Scandinavia.

In general, however, it can be said that, despite the changes mentioned, the Roman technological tradition was still evident in the glass production of western Europe till the end of the first millennium, when there was a definite departure from the ancient technology. Soda glass disappeared, evidently owing to a lack of the raw materials used till then, and the first potash glass appeared, in the production of which potash from the ash of forest trees was used as a fluxing agent. This technological change laid the foundations for the differences between the glass made to the north of the Alps and that of the Mediterranean area. In the north what was called Waldglas ("forest glass"), potash glass of a greenish colour, developed from the later Frankish glass, whereas Italian glassmakers and the production influenced by them remained faithful to soda glass.

As archaeological research shows, glass production in Italy was very

(text continues on page 25)

Glass, 3rd century (1—5)

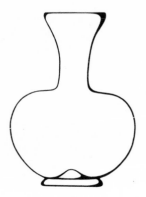

[16

1/   Alabastron of blue
opaque glass with combed
decoration of white and
yellow threads,
Mediterranean (found in
Capua), 4th—3rd century
B.C.

2/   Bowl of yellowish
glass, melted in the mould
and ground,
eastern Mediterranean,
perhaps Alexandria,
3rd—2nd century B.C.

3/ Roman glass,
mould-blown:
Beaker with almond motif,
eastern Mediterranean,
probably Syria, 2nd half of
1st century A.D.
Little bottle with stud
decoration,
probably Syria (found near
Mount Karmel), 2nd
century A.D.

4/ Roman blown glass:
Beaker of greenish glass,
Near East, 2nd half of 1st
century A.D.
Thin-walled bowl, ribbed,
eastern Mediterranean
(found near Homs), around
30—70 A.D.
Bottle of blue glass,
Italy or Near East, 1st—2nd
century.
Beaker with indented sides,
called a Faltenbecher,
Rhineland or Gaul (found
in Momaraie in France),
3rd—4th century A.D.

5/ Ewer, optically ribbed,
eastern Mediterranean,
3rd—4th century A.D.

6/   Frankish, furnace-
made, undecolourized glass,
France or Western
Germany, 6th—7th century:
Bell-shaped beaker,
optically ribbed.
Palm cup, optically ribbed.
Cup, the lower part everted

7/ Beaker with small
prunts and pincered rib
round the bottom,
Germany, 1st half of 15th
century

8/ Kuttrolf of green glass,
furnace-made,
Germany, around 1650

Beaker called a rhyton,
decorated with applied threads,
Frankish, 5th and 6th centuries

Drinking horn, decorated with
applied trailing,
Frankish, end of 5th
century — beginning of 6th

limited in the early Middle Ages. The great majority of finds consists of functional glass, which betrays a certain eastern influence, such as for instance glass found in Lombard graves from the 6th and 7th centuries. But the most important archaeological digs took place on the island of Torcello near Venice, where glass was evidently made from the end of the 6th and the first half of the 7th centuries, which forms a link between ancient production and the Venetian glassmaking of the High Middle Ages.

In the Near East, as distinct from western Europe, we can observe a clearer link with the ancient tradition. Not only did engraving and cutting of glass continue here, but also painting with lustres and enamels. In the 12th and 13th centuries, when there were extensive trade connections between the Near East and Italy, especially Venice, important technological influences penetrated the European continent from there.

Glass, 4th century (1—5)

Claw beaker,
Frankish, Rhineland, 5th
century

[25

Advice to Collectors and Recommended Literature

The first big publication on ancient glass was the three-volume book by A. Kisa, *Das Glas im Altertum*, Leipzig 1908. After the Second World War our ideas on ancient and later glass were added to by new and important archaeological finds and a systematic processing of important collections. And we can obtain basic information on the technology, shapes and history of ancient glass from the catalogues of these collections: P. La Baume, *Glas der antiken Welt I., Wissenschaftliche Kataloge des Römisch-Germanischen Museums*, Cologne, vol. I, 1973, A. von Saldern, *Glassammlung Hentrich, Antike und Islam, Kataloge des Kunstmuseums Düsseldorf*, vol. III, Düsseldorf 1974, Saldern et al., *Gläser der Antike, Sammlung Erwin Oppenländer*, Hamburg-Cologne 1974, which sum up the opinions of contemporary researchers. For the history of the Rhineland glass see the work of F. Fremersdorf, *Römische Gläser aus Köln*, Cologne 1928, and O. Doppelfeld, *Römisches und fränkisches Glas im Köln*, Cologne 1966, for questions of the developments in the Near East that of C. J. Lamm, *Mittelalterliche Gläser und Steinschnittarbeiten aus dem Nahen Osten*,

Berlin 1929/30. A handbook with dated finds of ancient glass, C. Isings, *Roman Glass from Dated Finds*, Groningen, Jakarta 1957, is very useful. There is a summary of present-day knowledge in three articles by D. B. Harden, "Ancient Glass, I Pre-Roman, II Roman, III Post-Roman", *The Archaeological Journal* CXXV, 1969, pp. 46—72, CXXVI, 1970, pp. 44—47, CXXVII, 1971, pp. 78—117.

The first copies and imitations of ancient glass date from the second half of the 19th century, when the Murano workshops made mosaic glass and fondi d'oro. The making of fake ancient glass still continues in Venice today. Around 1900 "ancient" glass was made by the Rheinische Glashütten, Cologne-Ehrenfeld, Loetz-Witwe, Klostermühle; and Tacchi in Frankfurt. However, contemporary primitive products from small workshops in the Near East are nearer to ancient glass. In Turkey reproduction of ancient glass is also made by blowing at-the-lamp. For information on these matters see S. M. Goldstein, "Forgeries and Reproductions of Ancient Glass in Corning", *JGS* XIX, 1977, pp. 40—62, and H. Ricke, *Glasprobleme, Kopie, Nachahmung, Fälschung*, Kunstmuseum, Düsseldorf 1979.

Glass from the High to the Late Middle Ages

The Carolingian and Ottonian periods, which in France and Germany brought a renaissance in many different branches of art and cultural life in the small circle of the royal courts, is a period of darkness from the point of view of European glassmaking. Apart from Viking glass from Scandinavia, England and Holland, almost no hollow glass appears at all in archaeological finds. All the same, there is mention of it here and there in church archives. For instance at Monkwearmouth in England, in the chronicles and correspondence of the Benedictine monastery of the 7th and 8th centuries, there is a passage concerning glassmakers from Gaul and later from Germany, who had to make window glass, pots and lamps for the monastery. The main centre of glass production at that time was still northern Gaul and the Rhineland, and from there glass was exported to Britain, Holland, northern Germany and Scandinavia. The forested area between Charleroi and St. Gobain on the French-Belgian frontier, called the Thiérache, was evidently one of the places where medieval production grew out of ancient roots.

From the 9th to the 12th centuries European glass production, like most of the arts and crafts, was most often connected directly with the monasteries, where the technical knowledge of ancient times was preserved. The members of the orders of monks and other church dignitaries, who were the only learned people of their day, were also the authors of medieval technological encyclopedias, dealing amongst other things with the techniques of glassmaking. All these writings are collections of recipes according to ancient sources, of which the most important was *Naturalis Historia* (by Pliny the Elder, A.D. 23—79). Both Bishop Isidor of Seville (560—636) and the Mainz bishop Hrabanus Maurus (c. 784—835) drew from this source. In other manuscripts, such as the *Codex Luccensis* (c. 800) and its later copy *Mappae Clavicula*, we can see how other knowledge from ancient times came back to Europe via Byzantium, Syria and Egypt. Heraclius, probably a Roman monk and author of 10th-century *De coloribus et artibus Romanorum*, summarizes the ancient and eastern traditions with information from contemporary Italian production practice. Besides practical instructions, we also find here echoes of ancient and oriental superstitions, recommending various fantastic mixtures such as dragon's blood, animals' milk and so on. In the 12th or 13th century a third book was added to this manuscript describing later production practice; it is thought to have originated in northern France. But the best source of information on medieval glassmaking technology still remains the three-volume book *Schedula diversarum artium* by Theophilus Presbyter, according to some by Greek authors, and to others by a Westphalian monk of the end of the 11th or first half of the 12th century. The second of these books deals with the production of glass, though of course it mainly concerns flat glass for church windows — the preparation and colouring of the glass batch, the making and painting of panes. It also mentions oriental techniques, such as glass engraving and gilding. Only two chapters cover practical instructions for making vessels.

There was a gradual advance in European glassmaking at the end of the 12th and especially in the 13th century when, thanks to the Crusades, which to a certain extent liberated Europe from isolation from the eastern world, there was a revival of trade and cultural contacts with the Near East. The Muslim world became a model for medieval Europe in many aspects, in the fineness of its material culture and the level of its technological and scientific knowledge, in the first place in medicine and mathematics. Syria particularly, which was taken over temporarily by the Crusaders, was able to contribute much

Medieval lamp (reconstruction from archaeological finds) — a type based on ancient lamps, found throughout Europe, Bohemia, 14th century

Ampulla,
France, 11th—12th century

Beaker cut in relief, called
a Hedwigsglas,
probably Egypt, 11th—12th
century

Enamel-painted beaker,
Syro-Frankish glass,
probably European, end of
13th century

Gothic goblet (reconstruction
from archaeological finds),
France, 14th century

to glassmaking, but there were also the influences of Persia and Egypt. The oldest medieval European bottles from the 11th and 12th centuries pictured in manuscripts follow models from the Near East. They are characterized by their globular bodies and long slender necks, and were found in southern France and Italy. In the 12th and 13th centuries all sorts of "oriental" products flowed into Europe as gifts from the Crusading knights, amongst them the famous relief cut Hedwigsgläser, called after the Polish princess St. Hedwig (died 1243); it seems most likely that these originated in Egypt, but some authors still doubt this, considering them possibly to come from Byzantium or even Russia. Enamel-painted cups were imported into Europe from Syria, marked by contemporaries "verrerie à la façon de Damas": the best known of these is the cup called the Luck of Edenhall (1250—65), now in the Victoria and Albert Museum in London and celebrated in Uhland's romantic poem. The centres where these richly decorated products were made in the 13th and 14th centuries were Aleppo, Damascus and Raqqa. After the invasion of Tamerlane, who destroyed Damascus in 1402 together with its flourishing industries and dragged off some 150,000 craftsmen to Samarkand, there was a drop in this excellent production. Syrian enamel-painted glass was of the greatest importance for European glassmaking, as it inspired the extensive production of enamel-painted glass in Venice, where the first glass painters have been proved to have been working as early as the end of the 13th century. A special group of medieval enamel-painted glass is that known as Syro-Frankish glass of the end of the 13th century, which can be seen both in European collections following archaeological finds (England, Ireland, southern Italy, southern Germany, Sweden), and also in illustrations of the period. This Syro-Frankish glass closely follows its Syrian models, but its decoration is rougher and technically less perfect. The best known example, signed MAGISTER ALDREVANDIN(I) ME FECI(T) and kept in the British Museum in London, has

Swabian coats-of-arms; other beakers have Latin inscriptions and are decorated with Christian themes. Once thought to be Venetian, this group of pieces is now attributed to a Syrian workshop at a Frankish court.

At the beginning of the 14th century, around 1300, European illuminated manuscripts show a new type of beaker with a bowl-shaped lip, decorated on the body with applied prunts and pinched ribs round the bottom. It is thought that these beakers too were imported at the time into western and central Europe. It appears from archaeological finds that the very important role of intermediary between east and west was probably played by southern Greece, where glassmakers took over many ideas from the Near East in the 11th and 12th centuries and developed them further. Very advanced glass production has been proved in Corinth, which was destroyed in 1147 by the Normans. Both the main medieval types of glass of the 14th and 15th centuries — beakers decorated with applied prunts and conical cups with an optical decoration — have their origins in Corinthian production of the 11th and 12th centuries. Glasses from the archaeological finds in Apulia in southern Italy (Lucera castle), dated 12th and 13th centuries, closely follow Corinthian models and prove that it was only via Italy that these types of glass spread further to the east, to the Istrian peninsula, and to the north, to Germany, Bohemia and Holland, where they appear only in the 14th and 15th centuries.

A further type of European glass, originating in the age of chivalry of the 12th and 13th centuries, was a goblet with a shallow conical or bell-shaped cup, most frequently ribbed and with a tall very slender stem, which occurs in archaeological finds in France, the Netherlands, Belgium and England, mostly in association with objects from the 14th and the beginning of the 15th centuries. However, French illuminations prove its existence as early as around 1300. But in this case it was evidently an Italian pattern, for the illustrations of similar goblets in Italian paintings and finds of fragments of similar goblets from Apulia are of an

9/ Medieval furnace-made, undecolourized glass:
Krautstrunk with applied prunts,
Germany, beginning of 16th century.

Maigelein with moulded ribs,
Germany, Rhineland, 2nd half of 15th century

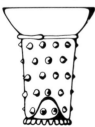

Beaker with applied prunts (reconstruction from archaeological finds),
Corinth, 11th—12th century

earlier date (12th—13th centuries) and are different from the majority of later west European finds in their perfectly transparent material. From Italy there originate two names for medieval German glass vessels that are still used in glass literature today — Maigelein and Angster. These are derived from the Lombard "miolo" (which passed into German as "miol", "meiel", via the 14th- and 15th-century Venetian "miolo", "muzolo") and from the Latin "angustus" (in north Italian documents of the 13th—15th centuries "anghestera").

So it is obvious that Italy played an important part as a link between east and west as early as the 12th and especially in the 13th century, through its contact with the eastern Mediterranean, through an important immigration of foreign, mainly Greek craftsmen, and by following its own tradition. In western and central Europe the situation was different. The decorative arts only gradually freed themselves during the 13th century from monastic life, and forest glassworks started to appear. These were mobile workshops that moved from place to place in the densely forested areas, moving on as soon as the forest was exhausted, and so they were often the vanguard of settlers in uninhabited mountain regions. There were especially good geographical conditions for setting up forest glassworks in Lorraine, Hessen, Thuringia and the Bohemian Forest. The forest glassmakers produced mostly Waldglas, greenish glass with bubbles and impurities in the paraison, caused by the minimum cleaning of the raw material. The greater part of the production consisted of window glass, made by what was known as the crown method, i.e. flattening the glass bubbles into a roundel by rotation.

Cup with vertical ribs (reconstruction from archaeological finds), Corinth, 11th—12th century

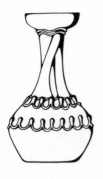

Kuttrolf with trailed decoration (reconstruction from archaeological finds in Plzeň), Bohemia, end of 14th century—beginning of 15th

Ribbed bottle (reconstruction from archaeological finds), Bohemia, end of 14th century—beginning of 15th

Both in ancient times and in the work of Theophilus a more difficult and more perfect method, still used in the Middle Ages, of producing flat glass was known, by blowing glass into cylinders, which were then cut and opened up flat. However, the crown method was much more usual in the Middle Ages. This had developed since the 4th century in the Middle East and soon penetrated to Italy (finds in Aquileia from the 4th century, in Ravenna from the 6th century), in Corinth it was used in the 11th and 12th centuries, and in Italy, in Torcello, around 1300.

Another typical product of the forest glassworks were simple bottles for medicaments, perfumes, for holy water, relics of the saints, etc. Medical purposes were served by urinals, in which urine was tested, vessels for bleeding and, with the spread of alchemy, many different types of distillation vessels, such as flasks, helmet jars, gas recipients and retorts. Chance illustrations prove that glass oil lamps, most often in funnel form, were currently made from ancient times up till the 15th century. Here it was evidently the Church that was responsible for continuity. Vessels in the form of a phallus follow another ancient tradition, being made mainly on the former territory of the Roman Empire — in today's Italy, Rhineland, France, Belgium and the Alpine countries, wherever folk superstitions connected with the ancient fertility cult continued.

A very popular vessel in the Middle Ages was a drinking bottle with a neck of three to five intertwined tubes, which was especially widespread in Germany, where it was called a Kuttrolf or sometimes Angster. They derived from Syrian models. However, in ancient times such vessels were used as perfume sprinklers, and in southern Europe they maintained this function in the Middle Ages and the Renaissance. The first mention is made of Kuttrolf in Germany in 1220 in the epic *Willehalm*, as a "gutturnium" for wine (from the Latin "gutta", a drop). Kuttrolfs have been found in France as well in the 14th century, and in the 16th and 17th centuries they were made in Venice: but nowhere were they so popular as in Germany,

where Kuttrolfs were mass produced in Spessart as early as 1409. Kuttrolfs were commonly used as bottles for wine and spirits in central Europe far into the 17th century, and even in the 18th and 19th centuries in folk glass. In the Middle Ages Kuttrolfs always had a globular body and a cup-like wide mouth, their necks are twisted freely and artistically.

In the late Middle Ages further types of functional bottles, pear-shaped and double-cone, were made in Germany. They mostly come from the central Rhineland, from the end of the 15th and beginning of the 16th centuries.

It is clear from medieval pictures of dining tables (such as for instance pictures of the Last Supper, scenes from the lives of the saints and court scenes from epics about knights or morality tales) that people often drank from bottles at table. Drinking glasses were of course known in the early Middle Ages, but it was only in the 13th and 14th centuries that their production became more widespread. In Germany and Bohemia we find no Gothic goblets on slender stems, known from Italy and the west. The oldest cups of hemispherical shape, decorated with applied trails, date from the 13th century and evidently follow the ancient and Frankish traditions. Much more important however is the type that came from the eastern Mediterranean tradition; that is beakers with a bowl-shaped or everted lip, decorated with applied prunts, which occur in Germany and Bohemia, and also in Holland and what is now Yugoslavia in the 14th and 15th centuries. In the second half of the 15th century these beakers became the well-known Krautstrunk, barrel-shaped beakers with big plastic prunts and bowl-shaped lips. This change occurred first in the Rhineland district, where Krautstrunks were most frequent in the 15th and first half of the 16th centuries, and where their gradual change of form continued during the 16th century till they became Römers. Around 1500 in the Rhineland big prunts were also used on tall cylindrical beakers, often with a trellised foot, and on Scheuers, low barrel-shaped cups with a handle,

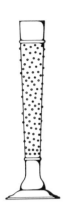

Fluted beaker with small applied decorations, known as a Bohemian type beaker, Bohemia – 2nd half of 14th – beginning of 15th century

Beaker with applied ribs and cobalt decoration (reconstruction from archaeological finds in Prague), Bohemia, 2nd half of 14th century

the form of which derives from models in metal. A decoration of small prunts appeared as early as the second half of the 14th century on very tall, slender, slightly conical beakers, given the name of "Bohemian type beakers", as their occurrence was first seen in Bohemian illuminated manuscripts and in numerous archaeological finds. This type of fluted beaker persisted during the 15th century not only in Bohemia but also in Germany, as can be seen from 15th century illustrations and finds in the counties of the German knights around Elbing and Königsberg. At the end of the 15th century what were called Stangenglas and Keulenglas were developed from them, which were decorated with horizontal ribs and trails and from which the big cylindrical and conical Renaissance and Baroque beakers derived.

Another type of table glass very widespread in Germany were the low Maigeleins, decorated with optical ribbing or a network and similar to models from the eastern Mediterranean. As can be seen from pictures, Maigeleins were common in the second half of the 15th century in France and the Netherlands too, where Krautstrunks can also be found. It is remarkable that both Krautstrunks and Maigeleins (later often Römers too) were made almost exclusively of green glass. This tradition is no doubt the origin of the old opinion that green glass is appropriate for serving white Rhine wine.

A less frequent type of Gothic beaker are conical ones with a bowl-like lip. decorated with applied vertical ribs. They appear from the second half of the 14th century in Bohemia and are often decorated with blue prunts and a blue rib at the rim. A later type of conical cup with vertical ribs, which were mould-blown, came from Holland at the end of the 15th century and follow the Venetian examples.

Archaeological research, carried out after the Second World War in the Near East, Greece (Corinth), Italy (Lucera, Torcello), Yugoslavia, Czechoslovakia, England and elsewhere, as well as constant research in archives, keeps unearthing new and surprising discoveries about medieval glass, and these help to broaden and correct our knowledge of the individual characteristics of glass production in the various districts and their mutual contacts and relationships. These finds make it clear, among other things, that in the 14th and 15th centuries a difference was already evident between west European glass production, led by France, and that in central Europe, where Bohemia played an important role.

Advice to Collectors and Recommended Literature

Medieval glass has been preserved very rarely and mostly in the form of reliquaries belonging to the Church. Mainly it is represented in public collections, where important archaeological finds are also kept. The basic handbook for getting to know the typology of medieval glass is still the extensive work by F. Rademacher, *Die deutschen Gläser des Mittelalters,* Berlin 1933, which also quotes earlier literature. The development of archaeology after the Second World War brought a good deal of new knowledge, which is clearly summarized by J. G. M. Renaud, "Das Hohlglas des Mittelalters unter besonderer Berücksichtigung der neuesten in Holland und anderswo gemachten Funde", *Glastechnische Berichte* 39, 1959, no. VIII, pp. 29—33, and D. B. Harden, "Table Glass in the Middle Ages", *Rotterdam Papers* II, ed. J. G. M. Renaud, Rotterdam 1975, pp. 35—45. The following articles are useful for recognizing the production of different regions: D. Hejdová, "Types of Medieval Glass Vessels in Bohemia", *JGS* XVII, Corning 1975, M. Wenzel, "A Reconsideration of Bosnian Medieval Glass", *JGS* XIX, 1977, pp. 63 ff. L. Kojičová and M. Wenzelová, "Medieval Glass Found in Yugoslavia", *JGS* 1967, A. Ress, "Zu den 'Schaffhäuser Gläsern'

aus dem Kloster Allerheiligen", *Jahrbuch der bayerischen Denkmalpflege* 27, 1968/69, pp. 74—95, A. Gasparetto, "Matrici e aspetti della vetraria Veneziana e Veneta Medievale", *JGS* 21, 1979, pp. 76 ff. A wide selection of types of medieval glass is shown in the collection of W. Bremen in Krefeld, *Die alten Glasgemälde und Hohlgläser der Sammlung Bremen in Krefeld,* Cologne—Graz 1964.

In the Medieval Revival period a number of copies of medieval factory-made glass came into being, mainly in the Rheinische Glashütten at Cologne-Ehrenfeld. But the main region where counterfeit medieval glass came from is the Tyrol. Sometimes these counterfeits are easily recognizable, while sometimes the collector may be confused by their artificially weathered and old-looking surface. Besides mass produced copies there are fakes blown at-the-lamp. From the point of view of craftsmanship there are very good imitations of enamel-painted Islamic glass lamps from the 13th and 14th centuries, made by Brocard and Imberton in the second half of the 19th century in Paris (cf. H. Ricke, *Glasprobleme, Kopie, Nachahmung, Fälschung,* Kunstmuseum, Düsseldorf 1979).

Pear-shaped bottle, Germany, Rhineland, around 1500

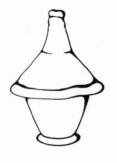

Double-cone bottle, Germany, Rhineland, around 1500

Beaker, called a Mörserbecher, Tyrol, around 1500

Venetian Glass and Glass à la façon de Venise

In the second half of the 15th and 16th centuries the Renaissance brought a great rebirth in the development of European thought and culture altogether. The cradle of this rebirth was Italy, founded on the spiritual heritage of ancient Greece and Rome and radiating its influence throughout the whole of 16th-century Europe. Venice was by no means one of the most progressive artistic and cultural centres in Italy. It was a city of enterprising, indeed grasping merchants and sailors, a city that, thanks to its fleet, ruled European trade with the east in the Middle Ages. Venice achieved its unique artistic character only at the end of the 15th century, at a time when its political power was waning and its economic prosperity dangerously threatened by the loss of the majority of its eastern dominions. It was only then that the Venetians started to rely more on their own means of production and their own forces. They concentrated their efforts mainly on luxury goods intended for export: woven silk materials, lace, maiolica, cast iron and, by no means least, glass.

From the beginning production and trade were protected, controlled and organized by the state. Various state regulations and statutes, preserved in the archives, are an important source for the history of Venetian glassmaking. The first of these is the Capitolare of 1271, a kind of agreement between the state and the glassmakers to regulate the running of the glassworks. A further extension of these rules is the Mariegola (Madre Regola) of 1441. We know from the Capitolare that at the end of the 13th century, apart from mosaic stones, called tesserae, the main products were bottles for wine and oil, cups and glass weights. An important component of early Venetian production in the 13th century were glass beads, made from canes or tubes, and window roundels made by the crown method.

It is true that the first mention of glassworks in Venice comes from the end of the 10th century, but production seems only to have become highly developed in the 13th century. At that time evidently the Venetian guild of glassmakers was founded, and in 1292 all the glassworks were moved out to the nearby island of Murano. By the end of the 13th century the Venetians probably knew how to make clear glass and how to paint in enamel. The first glasspainter in Venice known by name is Gregorio di Nauplion (Napoli di Romania, active 1280—88), a Greek by origin, from the region influenced by Corinth. Venetian glass was probably exported in limited quantities to England and Germany by the end of the 13th century, and in the 14th century this export increased in volume. We know that in the 13th century there were other glassworks in northern Italy too, in Naples, Florence and, last but not least, in L'Altare near Genoa, where an important glassmaking centre grew up during the 15th century. As the glassmakers in L'Altare were not subjected to the restrictions by which the Venetian government tried to prevent the emigration of glassmakers and the betrayal of their production methods, the people of L'Altare became the main propagators of the new Italian fashion in glassmaking in the 16th century, especially in France.

Information on the history of Venetian glass in the 14th century and the first half of the 15th is very scrappy. Only in the latter half of the 15th century do reports in archives contain more facts about the production, which can be confirmed by the first preserved products that are undoubtedly of Venetian origin. These are enamel-painted glasses, the oldest of which can be dated to the 1470s and 1480s. The shapes of the goblets, cups and bowls are simple, basically Gothic, reminiscent of goldsmiths' work. The glass is usually dark in colour — dark blue, dark green, dark red, with the

[33

enamel paint in glowing contrast. Sometimes too it is violet or golden-yellow. At the turn of the 15th and 16th centuries a group of painted milk glass pieces was made, and also an occasional piece of opaque turquoise blue glass. The painted decoration is mainly figured — erotic, mythological, depicting triumphal and wedding processions or at least portraits of young engaged couples on medallions. In style they resemble contemporary Venetian paintings, the earlier ones Gentile da Fabriano and Alvise Vivarini, and the later Vittore Carpaccio, or follow the engravings of B. Montagna, A. Mantegna, the illustrations to the Venetian edition of *Hypnerotomacchia Poliphili* and Ovid's *Metamorphoses.* Enamel paintings of the second half of the 15th century were previously, without sufficient proof, linked with the name of Angelo Barovier, who was evidently an outstanding personality in his day (mentioned since 1424, died 1460). We know positively of Giovanni Maria Obizzo (active 1488—1525) and Giovanni di Giorgio Ballarin (active 1511—1512) only that they painted large quantities of clear and milk glass. The production of milk glass at the beginning of the 16th century was an attempt to imitate the Chinese porcelain received by the Doges and nobles as gifts from Eastern monarchs. By around 1500 clear glass predominated, decorated with medallions of simple animal symbols or heraldic designs. There is richer decoration on another group from the beginning of the 16th century, which includes grotesque motifs. In the second half of the 15th century glassmakers preferred brighter lively colours. By the end of the 15th century aventurine and agate glass (calcedonio) had been invented, and the technique of millefiori had been revived from ancient times. So had the typical Venetian Renaissance technique of decoration with opaque white threads embedded in clear glass, known since the beginning of the 16th century, when documents talk of vetro a filigrana. In view of the fact that in the 1530s engraving with a diamond point was introduced into Venetian glassmaking, for which Vincenzo de Anzola dal Gallo was given the licence, as well as unfired paintings with oil and resin paints, we can say that the technical development of Venetian Renaissance glass reached its height around 1530.

It seems that at this time its formal development was also complete, for during the first half of the 16th century the Venetian glassmakers passed from shapes taken from metal objects to the typically Venetian shapes, corresponding in lightness and elegance to Venetian soda glass. Thanks to their advanced sea trade, it was no problem to transport soda from Spain or Egypt, and so the Venetian glassmakers did not have to give up the traditional soda-chalk composition of the glass batch. The shapes of 16th-century Venetian glass come mostly from natural manipulation of the gather, and its proportions from mathematically calculated aesthetic rules of the High Renaissance and Mannerism. Decoration was formed by applied threading and trailing, with embedding, pincering or moulding carried out under heat at-the-fire.

The taste of the Italian late Renaissance suited clear glass (cristallo), decorated merely with masks, handles, raspberries and threads. Venetian glass became much thinner and lighter than in the first quarter of the 16th century, and so the vessels naturally gained in elegance. An example of Venetian glass from the first half of the 16th century are funnel-shaped goblets with a big knop and bell-shaped foot, and goblets with a lower foot stem and a hemispherical bowl. About the middle of the century a type of glass appears with relief decorated stems, blown into their final form in metal moulds with lion masks or festoons, used throughout the second half of the 16th century. Also the blue handles or wings decorated with pincered clear trailing or cresting applied on the bowl or stem continued to be made even in the first half of the 17th century. At the beginning of the 17th century the shapes and decorations became still more complicated, the stem was ribbed or complicatedly shaped, ribs appear again on the bottom part of the bowl and optical decoration was often used. The shapes of 16th-century Venetian

10/ Renaissance utilitarian table glass: Smooth wine glasses, Venice, 2nd half of 16th century—1st half of 17th

glass can be compared with designs for goldsmiths' work, known from the artists Pierino del Vaga, Agostino Veneziano, Francesco Salviati and others. We can find examples of later Venetian glass shapes in the drawings by Giacomo Ligozzi (died 1626) or in the *Libro del principe d'Este.*

Of course, besides cristallo, vetro a filigrana also belonged to the basic types of Venetian glass of the 16th and 17th centuries, i.e. glass with a decora-

tion of embedded white threads, forming stripes on the walls of the vessel (vetro a fili), or a network (vetro a reticello), or with a decoration of embedded, prefabricated canes, twisted from a number of threads, forming a delicate lacework in the glass (vetro a retortoli). The oldest report in Venetian documents on threaded glass comes from 1527, when the Council of Ten issued a licence for making glass "a facete con retortoli a fil" to the Brothers Filippo and Bernardino Catanei Serena. In the 17th and 18th centuries the old technique of combed white "feathers" (vetro a penne) was again used in Venice for both clear and coloured glass.

From the end of the 16th and mainly in the 17th centuries ice glass was made in Venice. In that time the Venetians again preferred deep colours, manganese-violet, peacock green and cobalt blue, and further developed combinations of threading. In addition they variegated the surface of the glass with plentiful use of optical decoration of ribbing and studs and returned to the idea of relief ribs on the lower part of the bowl. These tendencies are even more apparent in the second half and end of the 17th century. Marbled chalcedony and opal glass (girasol) again came into fashion. The shapes of table

11/ Table glass in the Venetian style, Tyrol, Hall, around 1550—1570/80: Goblet with optically ribbed bowl and knop. Smooth glass hollow with a baluster stem

glass and decorative objects were more imaginative. The pincered decoration of the goblet stems was exaggerated, plastic decoration often appeared on vessels in the form of opaque glass flowers, especially yellow, white and blue. Many objects were merely decorative, the utilitarian side being played down. Venetian imitation fruit comes from this time too. Important evidence in dating this late style of Venetian glass is a large set of table glass preserved in Rosenborg Castle in Copenhagen, acquired by the Danish King Frederick IV during his stay in Italy in 1708—9.

During the 16th and 17th centuries glassworks grew up all over Europe founded by emigrants from Venice, which produced more or less perfect imitations of Venetian glass. The Venetian government passed a number

12/ Covered vase, diamond-engraved and painted in cold colours, Tyrol, Innsbruck, around 1570—90

13/ Ice glass,
Venice and Netherlands,
Antwerp, 2nd half of 16th
century and first half of
17th:
Basket for ice and Humpen
with prunts

of laws intended to prevent glassmakers from emigrating and betraying production methods abroad. Yet undoubtedly many Venetian glassmakers escaped. A great number of those who set out adventurously into the world in this way were certainly not the flower of Venetian artists, and in addition in the north and west of Europe they encountered great difficulties in obtaining some raw materials, especially soda. Glass production in places far from sea transport and with no background of trade contacts mostly turned out to be disproportionately expensive, and so many of the glassworks for making glass à la façon de Venise, especially in central Europe, were only in operation for a very short time and most frequently ended in bankruptcy.

Nevertheless, the production of glass à la façon de Venise did take root

and develop in regions where there were social and economic conditions for it: regular supplies of soda and other raw materials, a market amongst the very rich population and a large number of Italian experts, so that handing down technical knowledge was not dependent on only a few individuals. This was true especially of the Netherlands and France, where the Venetians worked together with the Altarists from L'Altare near Genoa. In these countries Italian glass was made in the 16th century which is practically indistinguishable from the Venetian models. In the German-speaking countries a number of attempts at making this glassware are known, but with a few exceptions they did not last long. All the same, the fact that they existed undoubtedly contributed towards improving the technology of the local

14/   Ewer of cobalt glass
with applied thread and
optical decoration,
Netherlands, end of 16th
century

glass production, the composition and purity of the glass, and at the same time it influenced the introduction of new production techniques and shapes. So it happened that at the end of the 16th century more advanced glassworks in central Europe were producing not only furnace-made glass, both clear and green based on the local medieval tradition, but also glass based on Venetian shapes, such as wine glasses on bell-shaped, baluster or mould-blown stems.

The Venetians began to feel the grave danger of competition from the central European glassworks only at the end of the 17th century. From the last quarter of this century Bohemian glass merchants were a particularly strong factor in the European glass trade, as they penetrated with immense enterprise and energy into all corners of Europe. They beat their competitors both in the quality of their heavy potash-lime or crystal glass and new techniques of decoration, such as cutting and engraving, and also in the low prices of their products. At the turn of the 17th and 18th centuries Bohemian glass became so popular that even the Murano glassmakers tried to imitate it both in composition and decoration.

The first mention in the archives of glass "ad uso di Bohemia" is to be found in the accounts of a Venetian merchant in 1722, but the patent for making it was only granted to Giuseppe Briati in 1737 and after him to other factory owners. Briati was the last important personality of 18th-century Venetian glassmaking. In his glassworks this gifted technologist revived and perfected the technique of threading, which had evidently been forgotten in the second quarter of the 18th century, and he created a type of Venetian chandelier composed of furnace made clear and coloured glass, with many architectural and naturalistic motifs of leaves and flowers, rich with colours and Baroque fantasies.

But our chapter on Venetian glass would not be complete without mention of Venetian mirrors which, from the 15th to the 17th centuries were considered the best in Europe. They were made by blowing into cylinders, and the makers framed them themselves, thus creating the Venetian mirror — a Baroque mirror in a glass frame, cut, engraved or pinched. One of the oldest surviving examples is the mirror in the Museo Vetrario in Murano, with a heavy frame of ground plastic leaves, which became the model for a large production of simpler cut and engraved Bohemian mirrors of the second half of the 18th century.

In the history of Venice the 18th century is a period of general decline, following the complete destruction of its political power in 1718, when peace was concluded with the Turks which surrendered the remains of the Venetian dominions in the Mediterranean. Whereas at the end of the 16th century there were some 3,000 people connected with glassmaking in Murano, in 1773 a mere 383 glassmakers remained. At the beginning of the 19th century glassmaking in Murano had practically ceased to exist. It was only revived by makers such as Salviati in the middle of the 19th century.

Yet there is a legacy that 16th-century Venetian glassmakers left behind them, artistically one of the most important in the history of European glassmaking. The links between European glassmaking and the Italian tradition is shown too in the literature on the technology of glass production. Apart from articles in various encyclopedias, of which the most important is Biringuccio's *Pyrotechnia,* published in Venice in 1540, there is a basic handbook by the Florentine Antonio Neri (1576—1614) *L'Arte vetraria,* printed in Florence in 1612. Here Neri collected his personally confirmed recipes for making crystal and coloured glass. His little book became the basis for later theoretical writing on glassmaking, which is really translations of it with detailed comments. The first to translate it, in 1662, was the English naturalist Christopher Merrett (1614—95). He was followed by Johann Kunckel (1630?—1703), who was a much more important translator for the history of glassmaking, as he was not only a widely educated alchemist but also a practical glassmaker. His *Ars vitraria experimentalis* from 1679 is many times more extensive then Neri's orig-

(text continues on page 57)

[40

15/   Venetian enamel-
painted glass,
Venice, beginning of 16th
century:
Ribbed bowl with painted
leaf frieze.
Beaker with putti and crabs.
Ewer with emblems of the
Führers of Heimendorf and
Ebners of Eschenbach

[42

16/ Table ornament in the form of a ship, furnace-made,
Venice, around 1550.
Vessels in the form of ships (nefs) were made in Venice in the 16th century by Arminia Vivarini, but we know that they were still made in the 17th century and they are also recorded in the southern Netherlands in the 16th century.

17/ Venetian glass with
pincered decoration,
Venice, end of 16th
century—1st half of 17th:
Small goblet with handles
and applied ribs.
Ribbed flute.
Ewer with pincered handle

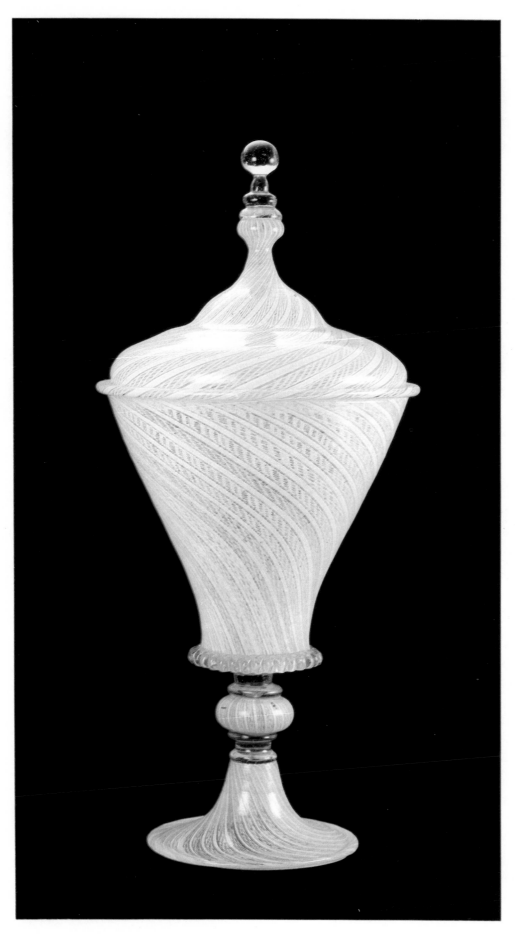

18/ Covered goblet of
filigree glass,
Venice, 2nd half of 16th
century (repetition of
a shape from the beginning
of 16th century)

19/ Venetian coloured
and reticulated glass,
Venice, around 1600:
Flutes with coloured bowls
and stems shaped in moulds.
Glass with manganese
layered bowl.
Two-handled bowl of
reticulated glass

[45

20/ Opal glass,
Venice, end of 17th century:
Ewer, cup and saucer

21/ Chalcedony glass,
Venice, around 1700:
Bottle with silver mount.
Cup with two pincered
handles.
Cup in the shape of
a Greek kylix

[48

22/ Late Venetian
enamel-painted glass,
Venice, perhaps the Brussa
workshop, 1st half
of 18th century:
Two bottles with Baroque
flowers

23/ Plate of milk glass,
painted in sepia, with
a view of the Church of SS.
Giovanni e Paolo in Venice,
Venice, Miotti workshop
(al Gesù), 1738—41.
The writer Horace Walpole
brought this set of plates
from Venice to England in
1741.

[49

24/ Covered goblet, enamel-painted, with the coats-of-arms of Hans Kleebichler and Barbara Fieger of Hall, Tyrol, Hall, around 1550

25/ Tyrolean glass, diamond-engraved, Tyrol, Hall or Innsbruck, around 1570—90:
Two goblets with motifs of the two-headed eagle, clear and green.
Humpen with unknown coat-of-arms and the inscription *Johann Sigmund von Freysing*

26/ Filigree glass from north of the Alps, probably Bohemia, beginning of 17th century: Mug with pewter lid. Humpen with bell-shaped foot

27/ Glass, diamond-engraved and painted in unfired colours, Bohemia, 1st quarter of 17th century:
Beaker with dancing couples, dated 1621.
Beaker with allegory Caritas and the Žerotín coat-of-arms

[53

28/ Little vase, enamel-painted, with leaves and birds,
Catalonia, Barcelona, end of 16th century

29/   Two jugs, furnace
decorated "nipt diamond
waies",
England, London, George
Ravenscroft, end of 1670s

30/ Winged goblet with
coat-of-arms, diamond-
engraved, called a verre à
serpent,
southern Netherlands, 3rd
quarter of 17th century

31/ Beaker of manganese glass with pincered ribs and prunts,
Netherlands, Antwerp, 1st half of 17th century

32/ Beaker with white, red and blue threads,
Netherlands, around 1600

inal work. Kunckel was translated into French in the middle of the 18th century by d'Holbach, and so the Italian Neri's knowledge became the basis of information on glassmaking once more both in the French *Encyclopaedia* (1772) and in the famous *Encyclopaedia Britannica* in 1797.

Strangely enough the earliest, though veiled references to Italian glassmakers to the north of the Alps come from central Europe; there is mention as early as 1428 of the glassmaker Onossorius del Blondio in Vienna and in 1486 of Nicolas Welch. The glassworks in Lublan, which were founded very early (working 1526—47), also came under the Hapsburgs, as did the glassworks in Trent and Villach (1486). But the most important glassworks in

central Europe were the Tyrolean ones in Hall (1534—c. 1615) and Innsbruck (1570—91); the former was founded by Augsburg businessmen, and the latter was under the patronage of the Archduke Ferdinand of the Tyrol himself.

The glassworks in Hall were started by Wolfgang Vitl, who is said to have summoned glassmakers from Venice. When he died in debt in 1540 the glassworks were taken over by Sebastian Hochstetter of Augsburg (1540—69). At the time of their most prosperity these glassworks had twenty employees, ten of them glassblowers (nine for window panes of which some three million were made a year, and one for table glass). Hochstetter sold his products in the Tyrol and in southern Germany. It appears from archive material that

[57

33/ Bottle with applied ribs, diamond-engraved, Netherlands, 3rd quarter of 17th century

Hochstetter first worked with Italian glassmakers, but later he employed only local labour. Yet the Archduke Ferdinand was not satisfied with his products, which probably mixed central European and Venetian design elements. In 1558 Hochstetter sent a large supply of glass for the Archduke to Prague, including enamel-painted Humpen, chalices, Angsters, bowls, tall glasses and double glasses. The last successful Augsburg businessman in Hall was Dr. Johann Chrysostomus Hochstetter (1569—99). His products were evidently influenced by the example of the Innsbruck glassworks, founded in 1570 by the Archduke for his own needs. There were several Venetian glassmakers at Innsbruck working, with intervals, with the exceptional permission of the Venetian Signoria.

34/ Goblet with a plastic
flower in the stem, called
a verre à fleur,
southern Netherlands,
2nd—3rd quarter of 17th
century

35/ Central European glass in the Venetian style: Winged goblet with lid decorated with eagle, Bohemia, Austria or Germany, around 1650. Covered goblet with a plastic flower in the stem, Bohemia, around 1680

Innsbruck products have been fairly well preserved, both in the Ambras collection, now mostly in the Museum of the History of Art in Vienna, and in the Bavarian National Museum in Munich and in other state collections. For after the glassworks had fulfilled the Archduke's orders it was allowed free sale of its products, and very likely Ferdinand often presented them to his noble guests at Ambras Castle. Their shapes are almost identical with those of some contemporary Venetian vessels, but they are larger, with rather thicker and less pure glass and the typical diamond engraving and unfired painted decorations that bear the imprint of a single workshop. The same decoration occurs simultaneously on cylindrical and conical Humpen and other less articulated beakers which are supposed to have come from the Hall glassworks.

Although Nuremberg is named in Venetian sources amongst the places where Venetian escapees could be found, there are no concrete reports on Italian glassmaking in the city itself, nor in the surroundings of Nuremberg. But in museums there are a number of goblets mostly with mould-blown stems and high-funnel bowls, decorated with cold painted coats-of-arms of the Nuremberg nobility dating from the beginning of the 17th century. Of course these could be the work of the Hall glassworks, which had one of its shops in Nuremberg.

During the time of Duke Albrecht V (died 1579) Bernard Swerts of Antwerp founded a glassworks in Landshut, Bavaria, which operated until 1580. In Munich itself Giovanni Scarpoggiato founded a glassworks in 1584 with Italian workmen, but this was not long in operation either.

There are diamond engraved and cold painted Humpen from the beginning of the 17th century which are related to Tyrolean glass, which are most often decorated with allegorical female figures copied from Jost Amman. One of them (in the Museum of Decorative Arts in Prague) bears the coat-of-arms of the Žerotíns, the most important Moravian noblemen of that time. Another of these beakers in the National Museum in Stockholm and dated 1619 is signed Nicolas Preussler, also evidence of its Bohemian or Silesian origin. Diamond engraved and oil and mastic (resin) colour painted glass was also made in the Rožmberk glassworks on the Nové Hrady estate at the beginning of the 17th century. Diamond engraving spread much earlier in Bohemia even than the first mention of it by the Jáchymov parson Johann Mathesius in his *Bergpostill* of 1562. Although Bohemia was only minimally affected by direct Italian influence, at the turn of the 16th and 17th centuries we do find here glass in Venetian style with mould-blown stems and embedded white threads, such as for instance a goblet of 1595 belonging to the Bohemian canon and humanist Georgius Pontanus of Breitenberg, found in Prague Castle.

In 1583 the Landgrave Wilhelm IV of Hessen summoned to Cassel the Venetian Francesco Varisco and the brothers Tiberio and Gregorio Frizer, to found a glassworks; the former had been working in Middelburg in Holland, the latter in Antwerp and England. In this glassworks, where the essential ingredients for melting were brought from Holland, some 20,000 pieces of glass were produced in the course of a year. But there was some difficulty in marketing the more elaborate pieces, and so in 1584 the glassworks was closed as unprofitable. It appears from a list of its products that the glassworks produced, among other things, filigree glass and those called Imperialgläser, which were identical with tall winged goblets of the Netherlands type, known as verres à serpent. Goblets of this type have indeed been preserved in large numbers in Löwenburg in Cassel, but there is some doubt whether they can be dated to the 1580s. There is mention of these goblets, with their tall stems formed by symmetrical twists of two canes with embedded enamelled threads and pinched decorations in southern Holland dated to the second and third quarters of the 17th century; and this also corresponds to the style of their proportions and shape and the date of their diamond engraved decoration. If this glass was already being produced in Cassel in the 1580s, then it was

Goblet with lid, furnace-made, with plastic monogram of Charles XI (1660—97) in the stem. Sweden, Stockholm, Kungsholm Glasbruck, before 1697

made without change for almost a hundred years.

Another place where glass was made in the Venetian style was Cologne. The first unsuccessful attempt by J. B. Calvart in 1607—8 was immediately followed by another by Antonio Sarroda (Saroldi) and Silvio Tensino, whose work also only lasted a year. As prefabricated canes for making winged goblets were found in Cologne, it is supposed that this glassworks made glass similar to that of the Netherlands.

Of course, the Thirty Years War caused a certain hiatus in the development of central European glassmaking. From this period there is only the Thuringian glassworks at Tambach, founded by Italians. A further invasion of Italian glass into central Europe only took place after the Peace of Westphalia. In 1650 a glassworks was founded in Styrian Graz and in 1655 in Kiel (Francesco Santino of Liège). Glass in Venetian style was also made in 1650 in the Buquoy glassworks on the Nové Hrady estate (Gratzen) in southern Bohemia. Italian glassworks were still being set up in central Europe in the last quarter of the 17th century, when there is mention of a glassworks in Dessau, founded by the Venetians Bernardo Marinetti and Lodovico Savonetti, which was working from 1679 to 1686 and made, besides mirrors, filigree glass and glass with unusually large coloured flowers. The last attempt, in 1696, by a Venetian, Giovanni Pallada, to found a glassworks in Berlin ended in failure.

There were also attempts to make Venetian-style glass in Scandinavia—in Sweden in fact — as early as the 1570s. The glassworks founded by Melchior Jung in Stockholm in 1640 employed Venetian glassmakers and made crystal and ordinary glass after Dutch and French examples. From 1676 to 1678 the adventurer Giovanni Bernardini Scapitta, known as Count Guagnini, worked in Stockholm. Scapitta, whose name is connected with the founding of the famous glassworks in Kungsholm, brought with him the glassmaker Jean Guillaume Reinier of Amsterdam, who may have been the maker of the unique Venetian style

goblets with stems bearing the monograms of Charles XI (1660—97) and of his wife Eleanora, probably made for their wedding in 1679.

In France and the Netherlands the situation was quite different from that in central Europe. Here glassmaking in the 16th and 17th centuries was founded on a broad production and commercial basis, the Italian settlers were numerous and the well-off class of the population ensured a good market. Here too, particularly in France, there were many Italian glassmakers from L'Altare. They came first to southern France and settled in Lyons, where enamel-painted glass in Venetian style already existed in 1511. Then the number of Altarists increased still further when in 1582 their Italian feudal lord, Lodovico Gonzaga of Mantua, became the Duke of Nevers. Thus Nevers became the main centre of the Altarists in France: indeed in the 16th and 17th centuries part of the town was called Little Murano. From there the Italian glassmakers extended their works to Nantes, Paris, Rouen, Orléans and elsewhere.

The French kings promoted the glassmakers of L'Altare to nobles and granted them patents giving them the monopoly of glass production and sale in certain regions. For instance for the Loire region the monopoly was held in Nevers by the Saroldi and Ponti families, in the 17th century by Giovanni Castellano and after him by the famous Bernard Perrot, who founded another glassworks in Orléans. There was another monopoly area around Paris, where Jean Maréchal was an important businessman, and after him Antoine de Clérissy. In Normandy F. Garsonet founded a glassworks in Rouen, and in the Nantes region the Ferro family. In 1615 there were some two or three thousand gentilhommes verriers in France. It seems that the Altarists mostly did not make luxury glass, but rather simple wine glasses and bottles in Venetian style. Their strength was evidently in their wide knowledge and experience in production techniques. Some of them, for instance Antoine de Clérissy in Paris and Jean Ferro in Nantes, made ceramics at the same time. Then the d'Azémars

36/ Opal glass in the
Venetian style:
Gadrooned goblet with ribs
and applied decorations,
France, 3rd quarter of 17th
century.
Two-handled covered bowl
decorated with gadrooning,
France or Bohemia, around
1670—80

in Rouen were the first to use coal for heating the glass furnaces (in 1616—19). The Altarists were experts in the production of crystal and coloured glass and must be given the credit for improving the making of flat cast glass. The Venetians on the other hand, with a few exceptions such as the Salviatis, settled in Prailler-l'Argentière since 1572, or the Mazzolao de la Motte family, active in the 17th century in Orléans and Rouen, were rather nomadic glassmen: we often find them sooner or later in Antwerp, Liège, London, Maastricht and elsewhere. Yet they were entrusted with the production of difficult pieces, such as verres à serpent, verres à fleurs, verres à bêtes etc., whereas the repertoire of the Altarists consisted of verres à boutons, à bagues, à olives, à branches,

à chaisnettes, à mascarons, à anneaux.

Then too glassworks in the Ardennes near the Belgian border certainly made demanding glass à la façon de Venise, such as the glasshouse in Mézières, where specialists from Antwerp worked, and that in Verdun, which belonged to the Bonhommes of Liège. Of course the goblets with snakes and flowers date rather from the second and third quarters of the 17th century. A speciality of French glass production were miniature figures of coloured enamel, introduced by enamellers of Nevers some time between 1565 and 1577. Fifty-two families were concerned in making this type of glass in Nevers. The objects were either blown at-the-lamp from pipes or modelled by pinching. Drawn glass could also be formed on a core of

[63

copper wires and green or opaque glass, or fused over a flame from various canes. Similar production existed in the 17th and 18th centuries in Venice, England, Holland, Germany and Spain.

In French glassmaking, great emphasis was always laid on flat glass for use in the building industry. In the Middle Ages the Lorraine region was the centre of this production, later Normandy. There was a great advance in making flat glass in the last third of the 17th century, when large windows and mirrors were needed for the monumental royal palaces. Bernard Perrot introduced making flat glass by casting in 1687, and his technique was further developed in the 1690s by Louis-Lucas de Nehou in the royal manufactory in St. Gobain near Paris.

Most important glass production in

38/ Cántir with optical
and pincered decoration,
Catalonia, 18th century

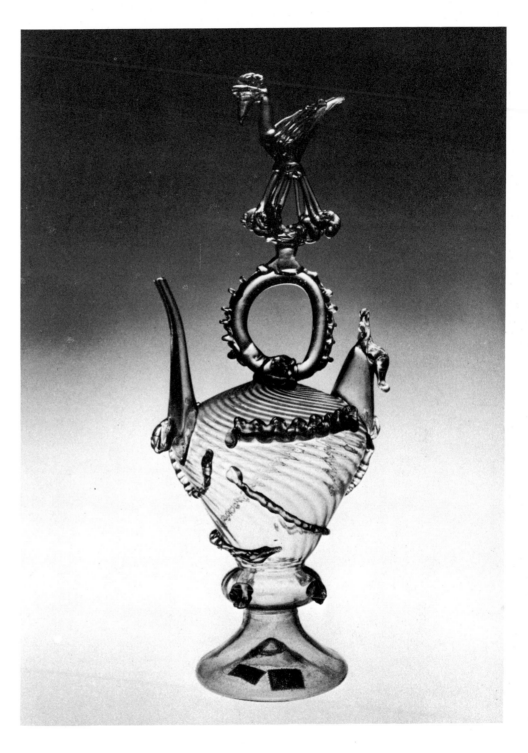

the Venetian style also existed in the southern Netherlands. In 1506 Englebert Colinet, a member of an old glassmaking family in the southern Netherlands, was given permission to build a glasshouse in Beauwelz near Mons (Chimey) and there make Venetian style glass. The Italian glassmakers who worked in glassworks belonging to local businessmen often had only seasonal contracts, so they regularly returned home and kept in contact with contemporary Venetian production. Antwerp, where the first Venetians settled in 1541, became the most important centre of glass production. In the 16th and 17th centuries it was a sort of junction from where itinerant Italian glassmakers branched out for other European countries. When Antwerp fell into the background after the Thirty Years War, its place was taken by Liège. Here the Bonhomme brothers opened their works in 1638, and in two glasshouses with Venetian and Hessen employees they made glass in both Venetian and German styles. They soon extended their works and were able to cover consumption in the Netherlands and western France.

The Netherlands production of the 16th century can hardly be distinguished from contemporary Venetian glass. We know that in the middle of the 16th century excellent threaded glass was made here in Venetian and German shapes, that were blown into relief moulds, motifs of plastic masks were often used and ice glass made. The well-known vessels in the shape of ships (nefs) were also sold. An invaluable source for the typology of Netherlands glass at this period is a catalogue of the firm of Colinet of Beauwelz in 1550—5 and the *Journal d'Amand Colinet* of 1574. From the 17th century we know mainly the big winged goblets (verres à serpent) and goblets with flowers, animals and other plastic ornaments in the stem, as well as goblets with two or three knops, all mentioned in the contracts of Italian glassmakers in the second and third quarters of the 17th century.

In the northern Netherlands, former Holland, the situation was similar to that in Belgium. In the second half of the 16th century there were Italian glassmakers in Middelburg (1581), Amsterdam and probably elsewhere. But it is likely that production only developed further after 1609, when the northern Netherlands achieved independence. Glass vessels in Dutch still-life paintings of the 17th century show that here, more than in the south, German-type vessels were used, especially Römers. In the 17th century tall slender flutes for champagne were popular.

The English production of Venetian-style glass is closely connected with that of the Netherlands, as the Italian glassmen came to England from there. The first of them are mentioned in 1549. A London glassworks with Italian workers, founded by Jean Carré of Antwerp, started operating in 1571 at Crutched Friars near Aldgate. After Carré's death the glasshouse was headed during 1572—92 by the Venetian Giacomo Verzelini, who came there from Antwerp, too. He was one of the few really successful Italian businessmen in western Europe. Altogether eight of his works, of simple pure shapes, have been preserved. They are decorated with diamond engraving which is ascribed to the Frenchman Anthony de Lysle. In the first half of the 17th century the most important London glassworks was evidently that in Broad Street, which belonged to Admiral Robert Mansell. At first Italians worked here too. In 1615 a strict ban was issued in England on the burning of wood in glass furnaces, and glassmakers were obliged to burn coal. The influx of Italians into England continued till the middle of the century. This, undoubtedly, had its influence on the character of English glass in the second half of the 17th century.

Spanish glassmaking of the 16th to 18th centuries combines Venetian elements with specifically local shapes, and in the south with ancient Muslim traditions. There were three regions in Spain, whose productions were strongly differentiated: the east coast region (Catalonia), the southern region (Andalusia), and the central region (Castile). The most important Catalonian centre was Barcelona, where enamel painted crystal, blue, purple and green glass was made from the end of the 15th century and during first half of the 16th. Its decoration is a mixture of Gothic and Muslim elements and later Renaissance ones too. Several precious examples of Barcelona enamel paintings of the period 1550—1630 have been preserved, in which green and white predominate. The decoration, mainly of plants, includes motifs of cypresses, orange trees, thistles, ferns, bells and lilies-of-the-valley. The enamel is often thickly coated.

In the 16th century the production of ice glass and threaded glass started in Catalonia. Combed decoration and a retortoli only came in in the 17th and 18th centuries. Then the traditional Catalonian shapes became very popular in glassmaking — cántir and porró, drinking vessels for wine with spouts and almorratxa — many-necked sprinklers for rose water. Cántirs espe-

Goblet with three knops, called "verre à trois boutons", Netherlands, 1st—3rd quarter of 17th century

cially were given fantastic ornamentation: to optical decoration and threading were applied rich fired decorations of high combing, clear or blue, and the figure of a bird on the ring handle at the top of the vessel.

In Andalusia there were glassworks in the provinces of Granada, Almería and Jaén. Glassmaking in the south of Spain, so remote from European civilization, was archaistic and shows direct links with Muslim traditions. Glassmaking developed there at the time of the Córdoba caliphate. From the 15th to the 16th centuries small glassworks operated there, and their style changed little up to the 19th century. They did not make crystal glass, but green glass of all sorts of tones, blue-green glass, cobalt blue, brownish black, purple and amber yellow, decorated with thick pinched combing, fibres, chains, shells. The most important glassworks were Castril de la Peña and María.

Castilian glass has the least expressive features. Even though travelling Venetian glassmakers came most often to Castile, the Venetian-style glass from Cadalso de los Vidrios is primitive and rough in comparison with glass from Barcelona. Finer glass in characteristic shapes was made in the 18th century at Recuenco. Otherwise the products of the numerous central Spanish glassworks are quite simple. In the 18th century they were all overshadowed by the royal factory of La Granja de San Ildefonso, founded in 1728, whose wares were influenced by English, Bohemian, German and French Baroque glass production.

Goblet in Venetian style, diamond-engraved, England, Giacomo Verzelini, engraved by Anthony de Lysle, dated 1580

39/ Southern Spanish glass:
Bottle with pincered free ribs,
Almería (María), 17th century.
Footed bowl,
Granada, 18th century

Porró, drinking vessel, threaded, Spain, Catalonia, end of 17th century—beginning of 18th

Almorrata—a rose-water sprinkler, with white threads and pincered decoration, Spain, Catalonia, 18th century

Vase, two-handled, of green glass with pincered applied decoration,
Spain, Granada, end of 17th century—beginning of 18th

Advice to Collectors and Recommended Literature

The earliest history of Venetian glass was written by B. Cecchetti, V. Zanetti, E. Sanfermo, *Monographia della vetraria veneziana e muranese*, Venezia 1874. The basic compendium on the history of Venetian glass today is the book by A. Gasparetto, *Il vetro di Murano dalle origini ad oggi*, Venezia 1958. There is much picture material and information in G. Mariachers's publications, *Il vetro soffiato da Roma antica a Venezia*, Milano 1960, and *Vetri italiani del Rinascimento*, Milano 1963. Results of post-war archaeological research have been summarized by A. Gasparetto, "The Gnalić Wreck", *JGS* XV, 1973, pp. 79 ff., and "Matrici e aspetti della vetraria Veneziana e Veneta Medievale", *JGS* 21, 1979, pp. 76 ff., and the archive research by L. Zecchin is also very useful. R. Schmidt, "Die venezianischen Emailgläser des XV. und XVI. Jahrhunderts", *Jahrbuch der Preussischen Kunstsammlungen* 32, Suppl. 1911, pp. 249—286, deals with Venetian enamel-painted glass, newer reports on painting on milk glass at the beginning of the 16th century are given by T. Clarke, "Lattimo — A Group of Venetian Glass Enamelled on an Opaque-White Ground", *JGS* XVI, 1974, pp. 22 ff., and R. J. Charleston, "Souvenirs of the Grand Tour, Lattimo plates with views of Venice in iron-red", *JGS* 1959, who deals with the 18th century. Late Venetian glass from the beginning of the 18th century is included in a collection at Rosenborg Castle (G. Boesen, *Venetian Glass at Rosenborg Castle*, Copenhagen 1960). Glass exported from Venice to England by Alessio Morelli in 1667—73 for the English Glass Sellers Company, represented by John Green (died 1703), is documented by drawings published by A. Hartshorne, *Old English Glasses*, London 1897. Older literature and also the latest publications on Venetian glass are summarized in the extensive catalogue of an exhibition in the British Museum *The Golden Age of Venetian Glass*, the author being H. Tait, London 1979. K. Hetteš deals with the problems of Bohemian glass in Venetian style, "Venetian Trends in Bohemian Glassmaking in the Sixteenth and Seventeenth Centuries", *JGS* V, 1963, pp. 39 ff., and so does O. Drahotová, "K problematice českého skla v benátském stylu" (On the Problems of Bohemian Glass in the Venetian Style), *Ars vitraria*, Jablonec 1979. Venetian style glass in the Netherlands is dealt with by F. W. Hudig (*Das Glas*, Vienna 1925), in Belgium by R. Chambon, *L'histoire de la verrerie en Belgique du Ile siècle à nos jours*, Brussels 1955, in France by J. Barrelet, *La verrerie en France de l'époque gallo-romaine à nos jours*, Paris 1953; "Un virtuose de la verrerie au temps de Louis XIV: Bernard Perrot", *Connaissance des Arts* 1958, August, pp. 48 ff., in England by W. A. Thorpe, *English Glass*, London 1949, in the Tyrol by E. Egg, "Die Glashütten zu Hall und Innsbruck im 16. Jahrhundert", *Tiroler Wirtschaftsstudien* 15, Innsbruck 1962. A very thorough monograph on Spanish glass has been written by A. Wilson-Frothingham, *Spanish Glass*, London 1964. The large collection of Spanish glass in the Leningrad Hermitage is shown in the publication by O. E. Mikhailova, *Spanish glass in the Hermitage*, Leningrad 1970.

Perfect pieces of Venetian and Venetian-style glass reach extremely high prices on the antique market today, whereas simple products of functional table glass are underestimated, though they are a model of fine design. Historical replicas and copies of old Venetian glass, mainly produced by the Murano glassworks in the second half of the 19th century and in the 20th, are very frequent. Besides factory copies, produced by Salviati, Compagnia di Venezia e Murano and the Rheinische Glashütten in Cologne-Ehrenfeld, the Josephinenhütte in Silesia and the firm of Poschinger in Theresienthal near Zwiesel, there are also excellent pieces blown at-the-lamp by C. H. F. Müller in Hamburg from the 1870s and Theodore Böhm in Utrecht from the 1950s (see H. Ricke, "C. H. F. Müller", *JGS* 1978, *Glasprobleme, Kopie, Nachahmung, Fälschung*, Kunstmuseum, Düsseldorf 1979).

Furnace-Made Glass from North of the Alps of the 16th — 18th Centuries

40/ Furnace-made central European glass:
Beaker with pincered spiral rib and free rings,
1st half of 17th century.
Beaker with pincered, spirally coiled, applied trailing,
around the middle of 17th century

41/ Joke goblet, optically ribbed, with the figure of a deer,
central Europe, around the middle of 17th century

Mediterranean glass production in Venice and other towns where glass made in the Venetian style was mainly of an urban sophisticated type, but to the north of the Alps geographical and social conditions were favourable for forest workshops. The glassworks, lying in the midst of widespread forests, had all the raw materials they needed close at hand: sand, in some regions especially pure sand, pottery clay to make the pans for melting the glass, wood for heating the furnaces and then for leaching potash, which was

used as a fluxing agent. In the wooded mountains of central and western Europe glassmaking was for long a country craft, relying on the traditional shapes and techniques. The products of these forest glassworks were more or less greenish glass, whose colour came from insufficient cleaning of the raw materials — both potash and sand. The decolourizing of glass only became widespread in the first half of the 17th century, up till then it had been practised only in the most important and advanced glassworks.

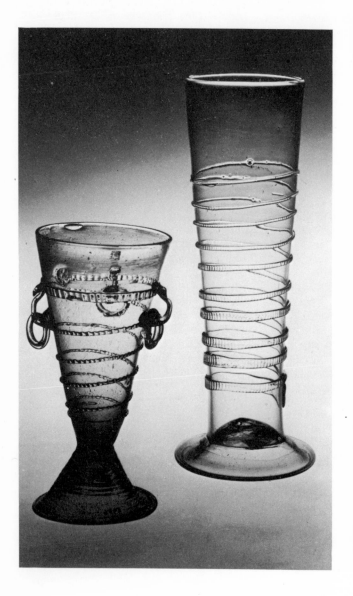

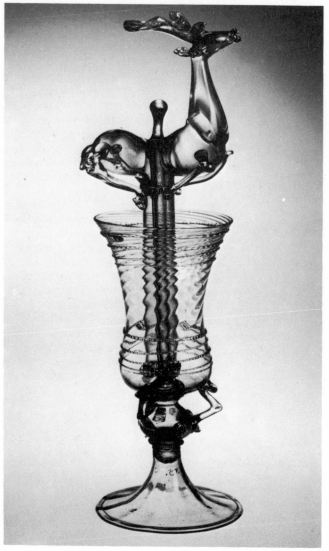

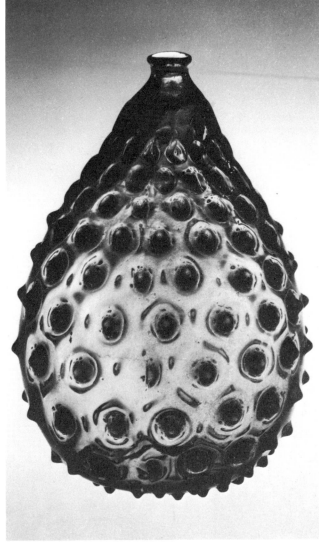

During the second half of the 16th century Renaissance influences started to penetrate to the forest glassworks north of the Alps, but of course in the different, less malleable material their shapes were changed. In comparison with the expensive Venetian-style glass the simple products of the forest glassworks were incomparably cheaper, and they suited the majority of their customers, mainly middle class townspeople, not only in price but also functionally and aesthetically. The popularity of this glass can be seen from the fact that even the most advanced south Netherlands glassworks produced what was known as German glass at the same time as Venetian-style glass in the 16th and 17th centuries, and this was modelled on the basic shapes of central European Waldglas.

The central European forest glassworks also gradually improved. The great spread of glassmaking north of the Alps in the second half of the 17th century and in the 18th is really the peak of the development of forest glassmaking, which at that time reached a higher standard of technique and so also greater productivity and flexibility in shape.

The main European regions of Waldglas were Holstein, the areas round Hanover, Hessen, Thuringia, Franconia, Saxony, the Bohemian and Bavarian Forests, the Tyrol, Bohemia and Silesia. Forest glassworks also existed in the Netherlands in the valleys of the Meuse and the Sambre, in France in Normandy, Lorraine, Picardy, Vendée, Burgundy and in Scandinavia in the province of Småland. In all these coun-

42/ Römers:
Small green Römer with a foot of drawn thread, Germany, 1st half of 18th century.
Römer of clear glass with a foot of drawn thread and raspberry prunts, diamond-engraved decoration on the bowl,
Germany, end of 17th century

43/ Yellow glass bottle for liqueurs, with optical decoration of lentils, Tyrol or southern Germany, end of 17th century—beginning of 18th

Beaker with applied decoration — forerunner of the Römer, Germany or Netherlands, 16th century

Beaker, called a Berkemeyer, diamond engraved, Netherlands, end of 16th century

Beaker, called a Warzenbecher, Germany, 1st half of 17th century

Römer with pincered rib and applied prunts, Germany or Netherlands, 2nd quarter of 17th century

tries the medieval tradition came up against the new Venetian inspiration in the 16th century. The medieval tradition was represented by beakers with big prunts; these survived in the 16th century partly in the traditional barrel-shaped form of the Krautstrunks, and partly in the cylindrical form of tall glasses (Stangenglas), which appeared after 1500. An increase in the size of the beakers was connected with a change in drinking habits. The big vessels, which were often handed round at table, had various decorations. The big prunts on this type of glass diminished in the second half of the century to optical decoration of relief lentils or applied trails either spiral (Bandwurmglas) or horizontal (Passglas), which measured off the amount each person was obliged to drink. An optical decoration of ribs, vertical or criss-cross, appeared most often on conical glasses, narrowed from the bottom up, based on the form of the Tyrolean Mörserbecher from around 1500. More rarely we find the club form, Keulenglas or Igelglas. Big cylindrical glasses became even vaster, especially from the end of the 16th century, when they were 50 to 60 cm high and sometimes held more than four litres. In German 16th-century sources this type is usually called Willkomm (welcome glass) or Luntz. The frequently used name Humpen probably comes from the 17th century. The stability of the Humpen is ensured by a trail or a slightly projecting base. At the turn of the 16th and 17th centuries a hollow bell-shaped foot was used, with a everted edge. The Humpen is related to the large mug mostly conical in shape, narrowing towards the top, or slightly bulging like a barrel, with a handle and often a pewter lid. It occurs from the end of the 16th century and during the 17th, fading into the background in the first half of the 18th century, to reappear in the last third of the 18th century as the most frequent drinking glass of the middle classes in both town and country. During the second half of the 16th century a bellied jug started to be made in glass, till then known mainly as a ceramics product.

Another widespread kind of furnace-made glass grew from medieval beakers in the 16th century, which was known as the Römer. This name most probably came from the lower Rhine and Netherlands verb "roemen", to celebrate or glorify. So the term Römer perhaps originally meant a goblet used for ceremonial toasts. And the Römer is itself of Rhine-Netherlands origin, a goblet with a big rounded bowl (egg-shaped or hemispherical), a hollow cylindrical stem and bell-shaped, usually trailed foot. This was the form of the Römer at the beginning of the 17th century, though of course we can follow the development of its temporary shapes from the Krautstrunck to the Römer since the 16th century. In Dutch paintings of the second half of the 16th century and the first half of the 17th we can see Römers with widely everted conical bowls, also found in the 1555 catalogue of the south Netherlands firm of Colinet at Beauwelz and in the *Journal d'Amand Colinet* (1574). In the Netherlands this type of Römer is called Berkemeyer. Early Römers are usually of a greenish colour, with egg-shaped bowls and instead of a higher foot an applied, most often pinched trailing. From about 1620 we find the typical bell-shaped foot made of a spiral trail, and after 1630 prunts appear in the form of raspberries shaped with a plunger. The size of Römers varies very much. English and Hessen Römers are optically decorated with ribbing on the bowl. Colourless Römers with wavy pinched trailing under the bowl and a smooth foot are probably typical of northern Germany and Sweden. At the end of the 17th century and in the 18th they were made with a high twisted foot and short stem, usually deep green in colour. Then these is the so-called Daumenglas—a glass with several indentations in the body into which the drinker's fingers fit. These are believed to have been made in Germany and the Netherlands.

The Kuttrolf is, as we have seen, one of the medieval bottles that have survived. The most usual in the 17th century were greenish Kuttrolfs made of Waldglas of a lobed or four-sided form. There are bottles of Netherlands origin of clear, blue, manganese violet

(text continues on page 81)

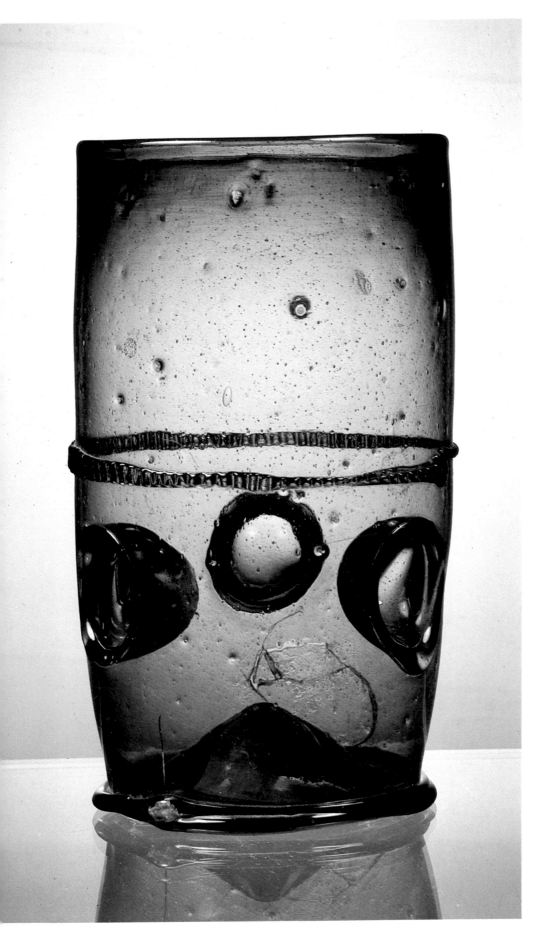

44/ Beaker, called
a Daumenglas, of green
glass,
Germany, around the
middle of 17th century

Römer of lead glass, optically
ribbed,
England, George Ravenscroft,
end of 1670s

Bottle with ribbed body,
mould-blown, called
a Kürbisflasche,
Germany, 2nd half of 17th
century

Pilgrim bottle, smooth,
flattened,
Germany, 17th century

[73

45/ South German
enamel-painted glass:
Humpen with the
coat-of-arms of Philippe
Oyrll von Hertogenbusch,
dated 1590.
Humpen with unknown
coat-of-arms,
southern Germany,
1570—90.
Venetian beaker with the
coat-of-arms of the Helds
from the 1st half of the 16th
century, which was a model
for these Humpen

46/ Enamel-painted
Humpen, with the
Adoration of the Three
Kings,
Bohemia, dated 1578

47/ Bohemian enamel-
painted glass:
Glass with free rings and
a hunting scene, dated 1594.
Jug of cobalt glass with
a scene from an animal
fable, dated 1592.
Jug with plant ornament,
dated 1601

48/ Enamel-painted
Humpens from
glassmaking families:
Humpen with a view of the
glassworks in Zeilberg,
dedicated to Caspar Steiner
of Volpersdorf by the
master of the glassworks
Christian Preussler,
Silesia, dated 1680.
Humpen with a group
portrait of the family of the
master of the glassworks
Martin Müller of
Schmalenbuch,
Upper Franconia, dated
1654

49/ Enamel-painted
Saxon glass:
Jug with St. George,
flowers and the inscription
George Ferdinand Sieche,
dated 1680.
Beaker with an equestrian
portrait of Johann Georg
III of Saxony, dated 1683.
Bottle with the allegories of
Autumn and Fire, dated
1670

50/ Enamel-painted
Franconian glass:
Humpen with a view of
Fichtelberg, dated 1669.
Humpen with the Last
Supper, dated 1660

51/ Goblet, enamel-painted, with parable of the Good Shepherd, Bohemia or Silesia, dated 1767

French glass, 18th century
(1—3)

or dark green glass with a tall slender neck and a spherical body from the third quarter of the 17th century, sometimes decorated with applied pinched ribs or a handle. A variation of these is the German gourd-shaped bottle or calabash (Kürbisflasche) with relief ribs, which can also be dated to around the middle of the 17th century. Towards the end of the 17th century and in the 18th jugs for wine became more widespread, mostly in shapes based on ceramic jugs with a tall narrow neck (Enghalskrug). Flattened smooth pilgrim flasks of a lenticular shape with a tall slender neck can be dated to the 16th and 17th centuries. But really numerous are simple every day bottles for spirits, of clear or coloured glass (green, blue, honey yellow and manganese violet); they have an optical decoration and come from the 17th and 18th centuries. Among them too are barrels belted with applied ribs, originating from the turn of the 16th and 17th centuries.

Some shapes of furnace-made glass are clearly inspired by Venetian examples. Among these are beakers with little rings which hang freely from applied glass loops and which tinkle on the bowl, and these occur in clear and greenish glass in the first half of the 17th century, both in central and western Europe. Also of Venetian origin is a motif of chequered trailing, which is made by reblowing the paraison with a spirally applied trail into a ribbed mould. Beakers with this decoration have been considered as Spessart Spechters, but it is clear that vessels of this type were made in Hall, in the Netherlands, Thuringia and Bohemia. Another decorative motif of Venetian origin used in factory-made glass north of the Alps are relief ribs gathered into rhomboids. We find these in Venice, where they derive from the Syrian tradition, at the end of the 15th century, but north of the Alps they are a favourite motif in the second half of the 17th century.

In the course of time too so-called joke glasses came into the folk tradition, also based on Venetian ideas. In sources from the second half of the 16th and 17th centuries there is frequent mention of cups and bottles in the form of female figures, bears, pigs, mice, owls, pistols, trumpets, boots etc. We can still find these forms in the 18th and 19th centuries. A special group is formed by glass with a reticulated decoration of drawn threads, based on later types of glass in the Venetian style of the second half of the 17th century. Here too belong delightful little jugs with thread-covered mouths and tubular handles, bowls, baskets and sprinklers with reticulated walls. This type of glass is to be found at the same time in Italy, Belgium and France, and also in Bohemia and elsewhere at the end of the 17th century and in the 18th.

Advice to Collectors and Recommended Literature

Furnace-made glass of this period is mostly a less demanding production for the broad mass of the people. At first it still follows medieval patterns, later Venetian Renaissance elements are incorporated.

The glass is usually more or less greenish, but at the end of the 17th century and in the 18th wares are almost always decolourized or coloured. Though not so noble in either shape or material as contemporary luxury glass, it has the charm and value of the anonymous simple country glassmakers, who had a great feeling for the material and a sound technique of work at the glass furnace. From this point of view historical factory-made glass is dealt with by W. Dexel, *Deutsches Handwerksgut,* Berlin 1939; *Glas, Werkstoff und Form,* Ravensburg 1950; *Das Hausgerät*

Mitteleuropas, Wesen und Wandel der Formen in 2 Jahrtausenden, Brunswick 1962. The studies by A. E. Theuerkauff-Liederwald ("Der Römer, Studien zu einer Glasform", I, *JGS* X, 1968, pp. 114—155; II, *JGS* XI, 1969, pp. 43—69) on Römers are an example of a thorough study of the development of one glass form.

52/ Covered mug with the Madonna on the moon—Assunta and Schürer coat-of-arms, Bohemia, dated 1647

Enamel-Painted Glass of the 16th—18th Centuries

Central European enamel-painted glass was directly inspired by imports of Venetian glass. The fine glasses and goblets supplied by Venetian glassmakers to the richest families in central Europe at the end of the 15th century and in the first third of the 16th were imitated in southern Germany. Humpen that have been preserved with coats-of-arms of the patrician and noble houses copy their Italian predecessors both in shape and also in the decorations of coats-of-arms and golden borders with engraved fish-scale motifs and several lines of enamel dots. Occasionally they are decorated with figures of lords and ladies in period costume. They are larger than their Venetian models, corresponding to the local drinking habits, and are usually cylindrical in shape, following the local tradition. The first products of this type are dated to the middle of the 1550s, the last to the period around 1590. We still do not know where they were made, though one of the likely places is Hall in the Tyrol. Some authors even consider it possible that they came from Venice, though at that time enamel-painted glass had long been a relic of the past in Venice.

The south German enamel-painted glass forms a kind of link between Venetian models and the typical central European Renaissance painted glass, which is mostly a much rougher variation of it. It was undoubtedly the brightness, intimacy, naivety and folk character of painted decoration that enchanted the noblemen and later the city artisans, for whom it was mainly intended from the 17th century onwards. Another decisive point was the size of the vessels, which gave plenty of space for painting. The main types of vessels on which enamel painting was done in central Europe were Humpen, from which people drank toasts round the table on festive occasions, weddings, guild meetings etc., mugs for beer and later four-sided bottles. Only exceptionally do we find enamel-painted glass in Venetian shapes amongst the examples preserved.

In the south German patrician environment enamel-painted decoration mostly consisted of heraldic motifs till the end of the 16th century, but in Bohemia there was a wide range of subjects for painted glass. The first mention of enamel-painted glass being made in Bohemia comes in 1561, when Archduke Ferdinand of the Tyrol ordered some from Sigmund Berka of Dubá. The latter was the owner of the Sloup estate in northern Bohemia, where a glasshouse had existed since 1530 at Falknov, founded by Paul Schürer of Aschberg in the Saxon Ore Mountains, and so we can probably ascribe the beginnings of enamel painting on glass in Bohemia to this glassworks. Another foundry belonging to Schürer near Zásada (Labau) existed in the Jizera Mountains in 1558. The Eulenhütte between Blatná and Nejdek in north-west Bohemia were especially important, and about 1540 Christoph Schürer introduced cobalt glass there. The later Schürers' glassworks in Broumy near Křivoklát probably supplied glass to Prague Castle around 1600. All these glassworks and later others as well used enamel painting to a great extent, and it spread widely in Bohemia from the 1570s. At that time too an important centre for refining glass originated in northern Bohemia around the glassworks on the Vartemberk estates (Chřibská, Česká Kamenice estate) and that of the Berkas of Dubá (the Falknov works on the Sloup estates, mentioned above). We can imagine what this north Bohemian painted glass looked like from material in the archives of the Brandenburg glassworks at Grimnitz, founded by the Elector Joachim Friedrich; this was put into operation by foreman Martin Friedrich of Chřibská in 1601/2, with five other Bohemian glassmakers, one of whom was a glass painter. In the accounts we find glasses bearing the imperial eagle, various coats-of-arms, emblems with the apostles, the Ages of

Man and the Electors, and also glasses with Landsknechts (mercenary soldiers), the Saviour and allegorical figures of women.

According to the dated pieces we can judge that all these themes on enamel-painted glass originated first in Bohemia and only later spread to other central European regions. First came glasses called Reichsadlerhumpen, with the two-headed imperial eagle. The earliest dated example is from 1571, the last from the 1740s. This idealized picture of the Roman Empire as a united organic whole under the rule of the Hapsburg Emperors originated as early as the end of the 15th century, at the time of Maxmilian I; and this is the time of the first graphic representation of the imperial eagle. The whole empire is symbolized by 56 coats-of-arms of the representatives of the various estates, borne on the eagle's wings. They are arranged in fours, called Quaternions. According to the symbols used we can divide glasses with the imperial eagle into two types: the earlier ones with a crucifix on the breast, copied from wood engravings by Hans Burgkmair from 1507 and 1510, or their later copies, and later ones with the imperial orb on the breast, found on glasses after 1585. The greatest number of these glasses originated in Bohemia, evidently in connection with the propagation of the Hapsburg political ideas. In 1661 (1669) and 1683 they are still quoted in the statutes of the guilds in Chřibská and Sloup as a compulsory test piece for candidates for mastership. Pictures of the Emperor and the seven Electors were similar in content, also celebrating the unity of the Holy Roman Empire. The model for this subject goes back to Hartmann Schedel's *Liber Chronicarum* from 1493. The direct models however are Hans Vogel's (or Rogel's) wood engravings and one in Bartol Käppeler's edition from the second half of the 16th century. The Emperor is seated on his throne, on his right hand are the spiritual princes, and on his left the temporal ones. Glasses with the Electors standing were made mainly in the period between 1590 and 1610. No model has so far been found for a later variant of this subject — the Emperor and the Electors on horseback, found on glasses throughout the 17th century.

In Bohemia in the 1570s paintings of biblical subjects became very popular. We find painted Apostles, the Evangelists, Original Sin, Noah, Abraham and Isaac, Daniel in the lion's den, Jacob, Samson with the lion, Lot and his daughters etc. There are pictures of the whole Christian story — the Massacre of the Innocents, the Adoration of the Three Kings, the Baptism, Christ and the Good Samaritan, Doubting Thomas, the Last Supper, the Crucifixion, the Ascension. Mythological subjects, on the other hand, are exceptional in Bohemia and only appear quite late. Allegories were more usual from the end of the 16th century, but they were used selectively and in a moralizing context, such as the Ages of Man and Christian Virtue. There is a much wider range of morality themes, including Praise of Virtue, the Student Cornelius, the Power of Woman and a number of animal allegories, based on Aesop's *Fables* and other literary works influenced by them. The large number of glasses with hunting themes show what an important place hunting held in the social life of the 16th and 17th centuries. These subjects, freely taken from motifs from Virgil Solis, Hans Weiditz or Erhard Schoen, occur on Bohemian glass from the 1580s. A frequent design on the surface of Humpen is a diagonal net in which noblemen caught the animals they hunted. Genre subjects in particular have great charm, and these appear on Bohemian glasses of this period in large numbers. Musicians, drinkers, dancers and players of cards and dice, horsemen and soldiers are shown in a very lively and often humorous way. Around 1600 appear the first motifs of craftsmen and guilds, miners, millers, coopers, smiths and linenmakers. But these themes are only developed to their full extent during the 17th century.

The mere enumeration of this wealth of themes, apparent in Bohemia much earlier than in neighbouring regions, shows the importance of the Bohemian glassworks in central European enamel-painting. The Schürers,

53/ Beaker, white
threaded and enamel-
painted, with the
coat-of-arms of Johann
Georg II of Saxony,
wreathed in the Order of
the Garter,
Saxony, dated 1678

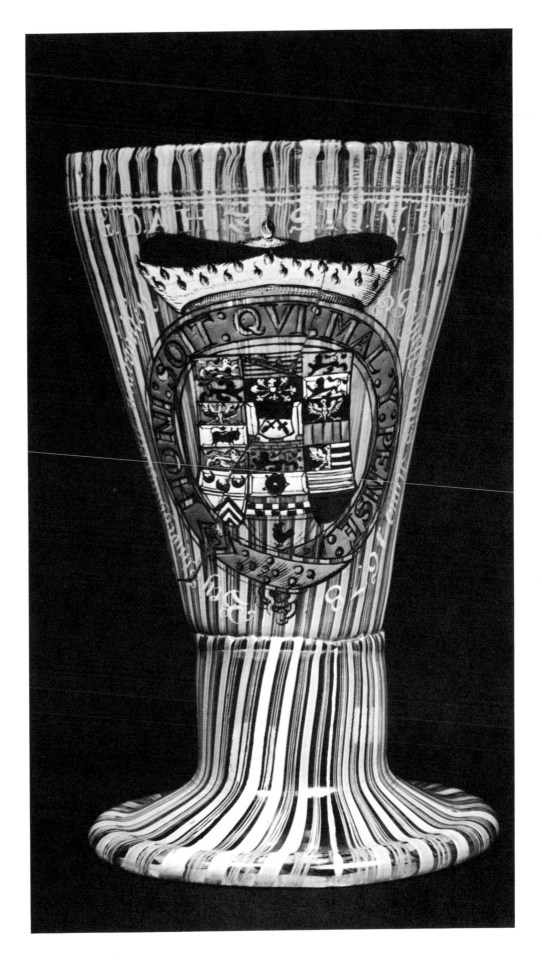

54/ Beaker painted in black and white enamel, showing the distilling of spirits, Franconia or Bohemia, around 1670—80

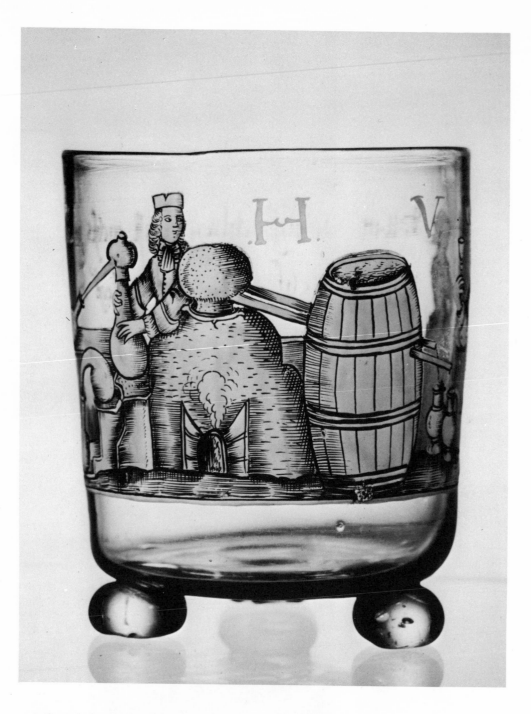

mentioned above, the Wanders and the Preusslers were amongst the prominent glassmaking families who settled in Bohemia in the 16th century. They came from the Saxon side of the Saxon-Bohemian Ore Mountains, and probably had a considerable influence on the technological and artistic sides of glass production not only in Saxony, but also in Bohemia, Silesia and central Germany. It must have been thanks to them that glass production in all these regions was closely related. The progressive technological standard of these Saxon glassmakers can be explained by the specific conditions of the industrialized region of the Ore Mountains. Ever since the 12th century this had been a silver-mining region, and later also produced tin, copper, nickel, lead and iron. The processing of these ores required technical knowledge and also led to the development of production and foreign trade, with Italy and Holland, amongst other countries. Experience of metalwork was carried over into glassmaking. Cobalt from the Ore Mountains was used for colouring Bohemian glass as early as in the 14th century. The first mention of its use in Italy comes at the beginning of the 15th century. Bohemian cobalt blue glass, decorated with enamel painting and dated from the 1570s up to about 1610, came from the Schürer glassworks. Sometimes these products are remarkably similar in form to the Netherlands Venetian-style glass, such as the mugs with spiral chequered trail decoration, and also bell-shaped everted cylindrical beakers with pinched ribs round the bottom and applied raspberry prunts, or goblets with a flared bowl and a hollow bell-shaped foot. In the 17th century cobalt glass was mainly made in Saxony and the Netherlands.

In Saxony the majority of the glassworks, such as Crottendorf, Breitenbach, and Jugel were situated in the Ore Mountains near the Bohemian border. The older glassworks, at Heidelbach, Marienberg and Aschberg, lay further to the north. The glass made here by the Schürers, Wanders and Preusslers must have been very similar to the Bohemian glass. Yet production of enamel-painted glass was probably not as great here in the second half of the 16th century as in Bohemia. Indeed the glass for the Saxon court was often imported from Bohemia. Perhaps painted glass was made in the Marienberg glassworks, where Georg Preussler, the foreman, is supposed to have made two Reichsadlerhumpen, signed G P and dated 1573 and 1577. More enamel-painted glass was made in Saxony only at the beginning of the 17th century, which also saw the original armorial Humpen and the first series of Hofkellereigläser, later made in large quantities for various Saxon castles, most of them decorated only with coats-of-arms, monograms and white bead borders. In the second decade equestrian "portraits" of the Emperor started to appear on them, and Saxon Electors or hunting scenes. There is a very interesting series from 1621, decorated with all kinds of animals. The painted glass includes threaded beakers and bottles dated from 1623 to the 1670s. There are very rare large beakers with views of the Saxon castles, such as Dresden (1638), Königstein

(1638), Hartenfels near Torgau (1688). The first two are signed with the mark of Christoph Löbel von Platten, who owned the Jugel glassworks at that time. Decoration with little glass beads was used in Saxony, just as it was in Bohemia. Around the middle of the 17th century Saxon glass painting suddenly improved, influenced by the immigration of Protestant glassmakers from Bohemia after 1627 and during the Thirty Years War. By then figured designs, religious, mythological and allegorical, were no longer a rarity. Often they are mixed with a strange kind of ideological eclecticism. Beautifully painted, almost naturalistic flowers are also typical of this period. Later Hofkellereigläser, from the end of the 17th century, are smaller, sometimes of white, blue or purple glass. There is a series of glasses that is typical of the first half of the 18th century, decorated with single playing cards and frequently with bands reminiscent of the furnace-made glass of the 17th century.

The Saxon glassworks were also the probable makers of big glasses with coats-of-arms of the salt refinery guild of Halle on the Saale (Hallorengläser). These glasses were carried, full of beer, during the Whitsun processions, so they are always dated. They gradually changed in the course of time. The earliest, dated around 1680, are club-shaped, broadened at the base. Above the coat-of-arms of the salt refinery guild, held in the lower part of the glass by miners, the procession rises diagonally across the surface to the house of the mining authority (Thalamthaus). A frieze is formed by a silhouette of the town of Halle. These glasses also bear Saxon flags, whereas the later variants from the time when Halle belonged to Brandenburg reflect this change in the flags too. The glasses, dated from 1682, have a large foot, above which the decoration is arranged in four horizontal bands.

Silesian enamel-painted glass is also very similar to the Bohemian production. In Silesia the Preussler family was the important one. The close relationship to contemporary Bohemian glass is shown by a white threaded beaker with the painted coat-of-arms of Hans

Engelhardt from 1594, now in Wrocław. Another very important piece from Silesia is the well-known beaker of the Preussler family of 1680, with a view of the glassworks in Zeilberg. According to the inscription, it was dedicated by the foreman Christian Preussler to Caspar Steiner, Mayor of Volpersdorf. The decoration was evidently done by Christoph Schieritz, whose name is given on the beaker as the painter at the glassworks. Volpersdorf lies near Neurode in the Glatz region, where in 1661—2 Johann Georg Preussler founded the glassworks in Freudenburg. The beaker evidently refers to his son, Christian Preussler. There also used to be other beakers belonging to the Silesian Preusslers, dated 1626 and 1727.

Bohemian glassmaking had links with the production in Franconia and Thuringia too. The glassworks in Upper Franconia were in the wooded area round Fichtelgebirge, the most important in Bischofsgrün. Here, too, several glassmaking families worked, the best-known of them being the Glasers, Wanderers, Greiners and Müllers. We do not know whether enamel-painted glass was already being made here in the second half of the 16th century. The first glass painters are only named after 1600. Franconian glass often strongly resembles Bohemian glass, and it can be distinguished from Thuringian glass only in some cases. Glasses that are undoubtedly of Franconian origin are those with a symbolic picture of the Fichtelgebirge with a view of Ochsenkopf, and also glass decorated similarly to Kreussen pottery. Evidently many painters worked alternately on pottery and glass, so we find the same subjects in both cases, for instance the Electors, the apostles and other Church subjects, allegories, hunting scenes, etc. Favourite motifs in Franconia were arcades and lilies-of-the-valley, reminiscent of Bohemian products. Here the tradition of Humpen with family portraits originated in the 17th century. Intricately painted Franconian beakers celebrating the Peace of Westphalia are almost unique. Later Franconian Reichsadlerhumpen are carefully painted and given typical borders broken

into segments which form intertwined lines. Glasses with guild and work themes are very similar to Thuringian products.

Thuringian enamel-painted glass was made near the Franconian border, in glassworks in Lauscha, Fehrenbach, Schleusingen and Piesau. The family names of the masters and glassmakers are the same as those we know from Franconia. Painted glass on a wide scale was made here only in the 17th century. Strong Franconian influences are evident, in the same ornamental borders, seen in the famous family Humpen of master Martin Müller of Schmalenbuch from 1654, probably painted by Johann Müller.

Bohemian influences in enamel painting reached as far as Hessen, which already had an old tradition in glassmaking. In the 16th century the Italians had a temporary influence there, but glassmakers from Bohemia and Thuringia were hired at the same time. One of these who was important for glass painting was Peter Hüttel of Kraslice in north-west Bohemia. One of the most favourite motifs in Hessen were hunting scenes, used in the second half of the 17th century both on Humpen (with a slanting network) and on green glass Römers.

In Brandenburg enamel glass painting was not widespread. It was used in Grimnitz (1602—7), having been brought there by Bohemian glassmakers from Chřibská, and in the Marienwalde glassworks, which were in operation from 1607 till the 19th century. Here too Bohemian decorators worked in the 17th century. But in spite of this the results were not excellent. One of the authentic products of the glassworks in Grimnitz that has been preserved is a marbled goblet with the coat-of-arms of the Elector Joachim Friedrich and his wife, dated 1602, kept in Grünes Gewölbe in Dresden. An example of the production in Marienwald are Humpen of the Brandenburg court printer Georg Schultz from 1670, kept in the Prague Decorative Arts Museum.

After 1700 enamel painting became gradually coarser and began to be more or less a folk art. Folk enamel-painted glass was made in Bohemia,

55/ Covered goblet,
enamel-painted, with
a landscape and strapwork
Dresden, Johann Friedrich
Meyer, around 1720—30

Bavaria, Austria and Thuringia. As a decoration most often relating to weddings, crafts or religion, it is so stereotyped that the characteristic features of different regions cannot be well distinguished or defined. Swiss enamelled glass too, mostly made at Flühli, is of a folk character. The French 18th-century enamelled glass is very similar to the central European folk production of painted glass. Probably this was mostly made in Lorraine, where a number of German glassmakers worked, such as the Greiners, Schürers and others.

In some countries enamel painting remained at a high level even in the 18th century. This was the case in Venice, where very delicate work came from the workshops of the Brussa and Miotti families. In Dresden, evidently in connection with porcelain painting, enamel painting developed too, thanks to Johann Friedrich Meyer (1680—1752), the Dresden court enameller. His work, in which ornaments of plant tendrils are linked with bands of landscape and figural motifs, are often carried out in bas-relief. A similar technique is that of decorating glass with gold relief on an enamel base; this appears in Dresden glass in the 1730s.

In Bohemia enamel-painted glass was revived in a new form around the middle of the 18th century. The work that has been preserved can be divided into two groups: firstly work painted in the style of the Hausmaler (freelance painters) mainly used as gifts on special occasions and souvenirs, and secondly painted glass that was originally part of a table or travel service. The decoration of this type is rather stereotyped, being confined to stylized landscapes enlivened with figures of Rococo lords and ladies, framed with a rocaille ornamentation. Sometimes they are painted in bright colours, sometimes in a combination of pink and white—en camaïeu rose. In the last two decades simple flower designs are more and more used, roses and garlands in pink.

In England too a delicate enamel painting appeared in the second half of the 18th century, attributed mainly to painters of the Beilby family, William (1740—1819), Ralph (1743—1817) and Mary (1749—97) active in Newcastle-on-Tyne. Their meticulous work, done on clear and white opaque glass from the beginning of the 1760s, cannot be distinguished one from the other. They decorated pieces made in local glasshouses with landscapes, coats-of-arms and inscriptions. Some pieces of their family production are signed.

Bottle painted in white enamel, England, Newcastle, Beilby, dated 1769

Advice to Collectors and Recommended Literature

The most extensive compendium on enamel-painted glass is the book by A. von Saldern, *German Enameled Glass,* Corning 1965. A later publication by F. C. Lipp, *Bemalte Gläser,* Munich 1974, deals more with folk glass. Questions of enamelled glass are summarized more briefly in the catalogue to F. Biemann's collection (B. Klesse and A. von Saldern, *500 Jahre Glaskunst, Sammlung Biemann,* Rastatt 1978). Among earlier literature dealing with individual regions we may name: K. Berling, *Die sächsichen Hofkellergläser, Neues Archiv für sächsische Geschichte und Altertumskunde,* vol. 21, Dresden 1900, E. Zeh, "Die oberfränkischen Emailgläser", *Cicerone* VII, 1915, pp. 343—364, M. Killing, *Die Glasmacherkunst in Hessen,* Marburg 1927, T. Ostertag, *Das Fichtelgebirgsglas,* Erlangen 1933. Of later works useful books are F. A. Dreier, *Glaskunst in Hessen und Kassel,* Cassel 1969, and S. Baumgärtner, *Sächsisches Glas. Die Glashüten und ihre Erzeugnisse,* Wiesbaden 1977.

In the second half of the 19th century there were numerous copies of enamel-painted glass. A particularly large production was introduced in the 1880s by the firm of F. Heckert at Petersdorf in Silesia (see F. Neuburg, "Gefälschtes Glas. Noch etwas über gefälschtes Glas", *Die internationale Kunstwelt,* Feb. 1936, pp. 37—39; März 1936, pp. 57—59; A. von Saldern, "Im Irrgarten der Kopien. Deutsche Emailgläser des 19. Jahrhunderts", *Kunst u. Antiquitäten,* no. 6, 1978, pp. 40—51; H. Ricke, *Glasprobleme, Kopie, Nachahmung, Fälschung,* Kunstmuseum, Düsseldorf 1979).

Cut and Engraved Glass
of the 17th and 18th Centuries

In central Europe at the end of the 16th century, just as long before in Egypt and Persia, engraved glass was revived, this time in direct response to the contemporary prosperity of late Renaissance Italian glyptics. The Hapsburgs in Madrid and the Wittelsbachs in Munich were the main customers outside Italy of the Milanese gem engraving workshops of the Saracchis and Miseronis. In 1588 Rudolf II invited Ottavio Miseroni to Prague, where he became the imperial and court engraver of precious stones and where he founded a big cutting and engraving workshop, in which his family worked till the 1680s.

The Miseronis did not remain alone. There were many other gem cutters among the artists that flocked into Prague, mostly of German origin. So at the end of the 16th century Prague under the Emperor Rudolf became not only the main centre of the late Renaissance Mannerist art, but also one of the most important centres of glyptics north of the Alps. So it is not surprising that Prague is linked with the beginnings of modern engraved glass. Caspar Lehmann, who came to Prague in 1588 from the north German town of Uelzen, received a patent for engraving glass from Rudolf II in 1609. And so for a long time he was honoured as the first glass engraver of modern times. However, a letter from Lehmann to Duke Maxmilian of Bavaria from 1608 shows that he had learnt to engrave glass and gems in Munich at the court of William V. This was the beginning of a search for Lehmann's teacher amongst gem engravers at the court of William V of Bavaria. The people best suited for this role seem to be Valentin Drausch, an excellent goldsmith and gem cutter who later stayed in Dresden and Prague (1582—5), and Zacharias Peltzer, who in 1596 also appeared in Prague.

Lehmann probably came to Prague in 1588 and, with a short interval from 1606 to 1608, lived there till his death in 1622. We know from the court chroniclers a number of details about his court services and pay, and also from the bills of the Elector's court in Dresden, where he found shelter in 1606—8, when he was temporarily dismissed from the Prague court. After Rudolf's death he was not taken into the service of Emperor Matthias, he gradually slipped further and further into debt and died in complete poverty. All he left was one signed work, a Prague beaker of 1605 with the allegorical figures of Nobilitas, Liberalitas and Potestas engraved for Wolf Sigmund of Losenstein and Susan of Rogendorf, according to a copperplate engraving by Johann Sadeler, which is on the title page of the publication *Schema seu speculum principium,* published in 1597. Other works undoubtedly by Lehmann are portraits of his Maecenas — the Emperor Rudolf II (Kunsthistorisches Museum, Vienna), of the Saxon Elector Christian II (Decorative Arts Museum, Prague), of the Landgrave Ludwig V of Hessen-Darmstadt (Landesmuseum, Darmstadt) and of Duke Heinrich Julius of Brunswick (Grünes Gewölbe, Dresden). A rock crystal goblet in a gilt mount, from the time of Lehmann's stay in Dresden, is decorated with a picture of Diana and Actaeon and is now also in the Grünes Gewölbe in Dresden. Further works attributed to Lehmann, such as panels with Diana and Actaeon (Museum für angewandte Kunst, Hamburg) and Ariadne and Perseus (Victoria and Albert Museum, London), and two panels dated 1619 and 1620 (also in London) are also connected with the Saxon court. The identity of the engraver of a beautiful panel with Jupiter and Juno (Grünes Gewölbe in Dresden) is still an open question. It was engraved after a drawing by Bartolomeus Spranger and obtained for the Saxon collection in 1590: it is true that it is very similar to Lehmann's works, but shows a very much higher quality than any other known works by Lehmann.

56/ Panel, engraved, with a portrait of Christian II of Saxony,
Caspar Lehmann, Prague 1602, or Dresden 1606

[92

In Prague Lehmann was probably acclaimed as the creator of the first engraved vessels, which took the place of the expensive cut dishes of rock crystal. The only pupil of his we know is Georg Schwanhardt the Elder, whom he taught from 1618. Even during Lehmann's lifetime other engravers probably engraved glass in Prague too, such as David Engelhardt (mentioned 1592—1614), the cutter of dies for the mint and crystal engraver, who probably came from Nuremberg, and Georg Schindler, said to have been in Prague in 1610—27 and apparently the same man who was received as a burgher of Dresden in 1628. In the records of the ceremony he is referred to as a former engraver of the glassworks in Mšeno (Grünwald) in the Jablonec region. The same Schindler is mentioned once more in the 1630s in connection with goblets formerly kept at Königstein and in Weimar, one of which is signed GS and dated 1640.

Georg Schindler was not the first glass engraver of this name to work in Dresden. As early as 1610 a certain Caspar Schindler of Porschenstein (in the Saxon Ore Mountains), burgher of Dresden, received payment from the Elector's court for the purchase of glass for engraving; he may perhaps have been Lehmann's pupil during his stay in Dresden in 1606—8. Another Schindler, Wolfgang, is given as a "Glas- und Wappensteinschneider" (glass and seal engraver) in 1613 to 1628.

In Thuringia too glass engraving is spoken of very early, mainly in connection with glass beakers for Wilhelm von Schwarzburg-Frankenhausen and Klara von Braunschweig-Lüneburg, whose marriage took place in 1593. The date 1592 is given only on the mount, which might have originated later and is not sufficient guarantee of the actual origin of the glass. The engraved decoration of the glass, now in the Metropolitan Museum in New York, is very close to that of the oldest "Tambach" bottles of the 1630s. The glassworks in Tambach, operating during 1634—9, is thought to have been the origin of a number of engraved eight-lobed bottles, of which of course only the earliest can really be dated to the period when the glassworks was operating, such as the bottle with portraits of the Swedish King Gustav Adolf and his ally in the Thirty Years War, Duke Bernard of Saxony-Weimar, given to General Banér (National Museum, Stockholm). In 1635 Elias Fritzsche and Johann Hess engraved glass from Tambach, and the latter settled in Frankfurt in the 1640s. Still earlier, in 1593, there is mention of a glassmaker Georg Weigand in the Thuringian glassworks in Fehrenbach, later quoted as a glass engraver.

Glass engravers in the free city of Nuremberg, however, are of much greater importance for the further advancement of the art. Lehmann's pupil, Georg Schwanhardt the Elder (1601—57), was the main personality there in the first half of the 17th century. But glass engravers existed even earlier in Nuremberg. These masters were all goldsmiths, like Hans Müller, Heinrich Knopf or Hans Wessler, who received a patent for engraving glass in 1613: his signed work portraying the Queen of the Massagetae, Tomyris, with the decapitated head of Cyrus is today kept in the Corning Museum. Georg Krig, "Glas Schneid", must have worked still earlier, as his portrait is in a painting dated 1583. All these unknown engravers prove that late Renaissance goldsmiths, who were also qualified gem cutters, played their part in spreading the technique of engraving glass. They mainly engraved seals, but on occasion also small panels for jewelboxes or cabinets, where they could with advantage use glass instead of the expensive crystal. In an illustration of a seal engraver's workshop by Jost Amman from 1568 we can see a light treadle engraving machine, which enabled the engraver to work independently of any other driving force for the engraving wheels. This machine undoubtedly meant an important step forward in the spread of glass engraving and was used until the 19th century.

The Nuremberg workshop headed by Georg Schwanhardt, already mentioned, who inherited the imperial patent from Lehmann, was for a long time the most important workshop of its kind. Not only did the father en-

57/ Beaker, engraved, with the allegories of Potestas, Nobilitas, Liberalitas, after J. Sadeler, and the coats-of-arms of Wolf Sigmund of Losenstein and Susan of Rogendorf, Prague, Caspar Lehmann, signed and dated 1605

58/ Bottle, engraved, with
the coat-of-arms of Maurice
of Saxony-Zeitz, his
monogram and that of his
wife, Dorothea Maria of
Saxony-Weimar,
Thuringia, dated 1655

grave glass in Schwanhardt's house, but also his two sons, Heinrich (1625—93) and Georg the Younger (1640—76), as well as three daughters and a daughter-in-law, who evidently engraved the simpler designs, such as flowers and wreaths. For many years Schwanhardt used rather stereotyped ornaments of slender plants in the forms of C and S, mainly terminated in sunflowers. Details of engraving done with a diamond point, characteristic of Schwanhardt's work, are landscapes with a lake, cliffs and huntsmen. It was his son Heinrich who was most esteemed by his contemporaries. Several works with calligraphically ornamental letters are attributed to him, and also work with large figures. It may be supposed that, as distinct from his father, he used mainly the classic type of tall baluster goblets, made in an as yet unknown glassworks after the middle of the 17th century. This well proportioned goblet of excellent glass, which the Nuremberg engravers favoured throughout the second half of the 17th century, is based on Venetian models, but lacks the mannered Venetian aesthetics in its size and the multiplicity of little collars on the stem. On the other hand it is strongly reminiscent of contemporary Nuremberg work in turned ivory and wood.

A contemporary of Georg Schwanhardt the Younger was Hermann Schwinger (1640—83), a very productive engraver and a competitor of Schwanhardt's. No less than fifteen known signed works prove that Schwinger engraved similar landscapes with ruins and shepherds or hunting scenes as did Georg Schwanhardt the Elder.

The last of the great Nuremberg engravers of the 17th century was Johann Wolfgang Schmidt, working in Nuremberg during 1676—1710. His forest landscapes with ruins are much more dramatic than anything so far seen in Nuremberg. He chose battles and skirmishes for his subjects, reflecting the troubled times and the dramas of the Turkish wars, and achieved a sense of monumentality in his spacious presentation of mighty trees. The days of war are also recalled by portraits of Prince Eugene, Ludwig of Baden, Josef I and Charles VI, wreathed in trophies.

Among the later Nuremberg glass engravers was Paulus Eder, active in 1685—1709. Only a small number of works are attributed to him, based on a signed goblet in the Germanisches Nationalmuseum in Nuremberg. Mostly he used thick chalk glass of unusual shapes, which he decorated with heavy Baroque swags of flowers and fruit.

The style of the older Nuremberg engravers comes to an end with the work of Georg Friedrich Killinger, active from 1694 to 1726. His hunting scenes are set beneath tall trees, his scenes from the city streets often refer to actual events from the life of the Nuremberg patricians. His works from the second decade of the 18th century approach those of his younger contemporary A.W. Mäuerl. His engravings from this period are deeper, as they are done on Bohemian chalk glass, which was imported to Nuremberg from about 1700.

Other lesser known names of Nuremberg gem and glass engravers, such as Erhard (1649—1712) and Christoph (1676—1732) Dorsch, show that our knowledge of the history of the famous Nuremberg glass engravers from the second half of the 17th century is still not complete. A single signed goblet of the beginning of the 18th century, with a portrait of a lady by Christoph Dorsch, is in Hanover. An earlier goblet, signed Adam Renneisen, is in Weimar. There is no mention of its maker in Nuremberg sources.

Painted faience and engraved glass have been attributed to Johann Heel, a goldsmith from Augsburg settled in Nuremberg, but probably he never engraved glass. On the other hand some relief portraits of coloured glass pressed into moulds can probably be attributed to him.

Thuringian engraved glass from the second half of the 17th century was dependent on Nuremberg models for form and decoration. This can be seen from the work of Caspar Creutzburg, engraver to Duke Friedrich I of Saxony-Gotha, whose engraved glass from the period around 1690, decorated with typical motifs of vines, is in the Veste Coburg collections. Creutzburg was probably apprenticed in Nuremberg and on occasion also used glass of Nuremberg type. Alexander Seiffard (died 1714), who worked in Arnstadt, was a contemporary. The same dependance on Nuremberg style can also be seen in Frankfurt, where the Hess family worked from the 1640s: Johann Hess, evidently the one mentioned in Tambach in the 1630s, Johann Benedict Hess (died 1674) and after him other members of his family. The most important example of their type of work is a goblet of the Drach family's from Cassel dated around 1670.

Bohemian glass of the second half of the 17th century is individual in shape. Goblets on tall stems made of several knops hark back to types of glass in Venetian style used throughout the first three quarters of the 17th century in the Nethêrlands (verres à deux ou à trois boutons), whereas glasses on three bun feet were modelled on gold-

smiths' work. Apparently the spread of this type of glass is connected with the revival of glassmaking after the Thirty Years War, when a number of glass-works were founded by Italians from the Netherlands or from Venice, who introduced later types of Venetian-style glass into central Europe. One of these was evidently the Buquoy glass-works in Dobrá Voda (Heilbrunn). Venetian-style goblets with several knops were made in Bohemia up till about 1690. However, their glass is less pliable, the balusters and knops are

mostly solid and relief ribs are usually applied on the bowls.

In Bohemia engraved glass devel-oped on a broader basis than in the other central European countries, as a direct result of the late Renaissance tradition. During the last third of the 17th-century glass engraving in Bohe-mia spread rapidly. Right from the be-ginning two main centres can be seen, both in northern Bohemia: the Jablo-nec region in the Jizera Mountains and those of the estates of Česká Kame-nice (Kamnitz), Sloup (Bürgstein) and

59/ Flute, engraved, with flower decoration and vases,
a German engraver working in the northern Netherlands, around 1660—70

60/ Flute, engraved, with decoration of sunflowers and animals, Nuremberg, around 1670—80

61/ Goblet, engraved,
with Bacchus putti,
a German engraver
working in the northern
Netherlands, around
1660—70

62/ Goblet, engraved,
with Athena and the lion,
Nuremberg, attributed to
Hermann Schwinger,
around 1670—80

Horní Libchava (Ober-Liebich) in the
Česká Lípa region, where even earlier
there were many glass painters round
the glassworks in Falknov (Falkenau)
and Chřibská (Kreibitz). This is where
the most important Bohemian centre
of glass decoration originated. Bohemian
glass decorators' guilds were established
in Chřibská (in 1661), Polevsko
(Blottendorf, 1683) and Kamenický
Šenov (Steinschönau, 1694). Apart
from these two north Bohemian centres,
glass engravers were relatively
rare. In south Bohemia they were to be

found scarcely in Vimperk (Winterberg),
Zejbiš (Seewiesen), Volary
(Wallern) and near the Buquoy glassworks
at the Nové Hrady estates
(Gratzen). Otherwise glass engravers
worked in glassworks only in exceptional
cases, often in the pay of the
north Bohemian glass tradesmen, for
whom they engraved glass directly in
the works where it was bought.

The engraved decoration of Bohemian
glass in the 17th century is, with
few exceptions, quite simple. The engraving
was shallow and dull, the sub-

[99

ject of the decoration most often primitive landscapes with incidental figures, the oriental motif of a bird and cliffs, or Chinese architectural or flower designs. The technique of glass engraving reached its height only later on perfected glass—the thick-walled Baroque crystal glass, which was invented in the last quarter of the 17th century.

The first attempts at producing a new type of glass came about in the 1670s in different parts of Europe.

Glassmaking north of the Alps, then sufficiently technically advanced, gradually freed itself from Italian influence. Lead crystal glass came into being at that time in England, where since 1612 there had been a ban on the use of wood for heating the glass furnaces. It was discovered by George Ravenscroft (1632—83), who, after a long stay in Venice, where lead was used in coloured imitations of precious stones, tried to make vessels of clear lead glass. Being meltable at lower tempe-

65/ Sweetmeat bowl, engraved, with flower and fruit motifs, Bohemia, around 1680

ratures, this was very advantageous for the English conditions, as work with this new material lessened the risk of impurity in glass from the dust and smoke of the coal. The first of Ravenscroft's products from the years 1676—7 suffered from glass disease (crizzling), but later the production technique improved. Ravenscroft's well-known sign—the impressed seal of a raven's head—was the maker's guarantee of the quality of the glass. In shape Ravenscroft's products—baluster goblets, jugs, Römers and bowls—were a mixture of Italian and western European elements.

The extent of French glassmakers' share in the new glass in the second half of the 17th century has not yet been evaluated. Their efforts were concentrated on the production of flat cast glass for the huge windows and mirrors of the royal palaces. Nevertheless, these attempts evidently brought new knowledge on making crystal glass too, and helped to lessen depen-

66/ Beaker, engraved, with grotesque ornament in the style of Jean Bérain, northern Bohemia, around 1720—30

67/ Goblet, engraved,
with a portrait of Charles
VI after P.H. Müller's
coronation medal of 1711,
northern Bohemia, around
1720

68/ Covered goblet,
engraved, with a portrait of
Charles III (VI) as King of
Spain,
northern Bohemia,
1705—11

dence on Italian tradition. It was in France that, among other things, the idea was born of the faceted chandeliers, on which pressed and ground glass pendants replaced those of rock crystal. The central figure behind all the new ideas was the outstanding glass technologist, Bernard Perrot of Orléans (died 1709).

In central Europe, i.e. in Bohemia and at the courts of the various German states, attempts at the production of a new kind of molten glass had

a different aim, based on the surviving tradition of Late Renaissance carving. The new Baroque crystal glass was to have qualities nearer to those of natural rock crystal than the Venetian "cristallo". It was to be thick, shining and hard, to enable perfect use of the glyptic technique—cutting and engraving. Late gem engravers evidently influenced the shapes of Baroque engraved glass—people such as Christoph Labhardt (1641—95), a Swiss by origin, active in Cassel since 1680. As can be

69/ Covered flute, cut
with printies and wedges,
Bohemia, about 1720

Ewer of lead glass, optically
ribbed,
England, George Ravenscroft,
around 1676—7

seen from his work in Cassel, Copenhagen and Moscow, he worked mainly
in relief, both in hard stones and glass.
A water-driven cutting mill for this
was set up in Cassel. Labhardt taught
the excellent glass engraver Franz
Gondelach (1663—1726), mentioned in
Cassel since 1689. It is certainly no
coincidence that similar water-mills
and similar relief cut glass are to be
found at the same time in Brandenburg

and Silesia. In 1687 a water-driven cutting mill was built for Martin Winter
(died 1702), engraver to the great Elector Friedrich Wilhelm of Brandenburg
in Berlin. But there are reports that
Winter made relief cut glass as early as
1683. In 1688 Count Christoph Leopold Schaffgotsch had similar water-
mills installed in Hermsdorf near Petersdorf for Martin Winter's brother
Friedrich (died before 1712), who

70/ Covered goblet, engraved in relief, with a plastic volute and the Schaffgotsch coat-of-arms, Silesia, Petersdorf, Friedrich Winter, around 1700

Baluster goblet of lead glass, England, around 1690

worked in Silesia. The Winters and their nephew Spiller came from Rabishau in Silesia. There are close links between the products of the Winter brothers and of Gottfried Spiller (1663—1728), who continued Martin Winter's work in Berlin. But a relationship can also be seen on comparing the relief cut glass from Silesia and Berlin with goblets by Franz Gondelach, who appears to have excelled all the other engravers mentioned. He was a contemporary of Spiller's, younger than the Winters. We still do not know the missing link that might explain these technological and formal connections. The supposition of mutual relationships between the three production centres of relief cut glass is supported by the friendly contacts between the employers and feudal lords of these artists: Count Christoph Leopold Schaff-

Goblet, relief cut, with the Hessen coat-of-arms, Hessen, Cassel, Franz Gondelach, dated 1715

gotsch carried on a correspondence concerning glassmaking in the eighties with the Brandenburg Elector and Friedrich III of Brandenburg (later Friedrich I), who married the daughter of Duke Charles of Hessen-Cassel in 1689.

Particularly thick and perfect glass had to be made for the relief cut glass. The most beautiful glass, sometimes yellowish or pink-tinged, came from Martin Winter's and Gottfried Spiller's workshop. It was supplied by the Elector's glassworks near Potsdam, headed since 1678 by the well-known glass technologist Johann Kunckel (1630?—1703). Under his leadership the Potsdam glassworks came to the forefront of central European glassmaking.

The process of change in the composition and character of glass took place on a very wide production base in Bohemia. We first hear of the production of crystal glass there in the 1670s. This term, quite common in Venice and glassworks with Italian workers, only appeared in central European sources in the second half of the 17th century, no doubt in connection with the spread of knowledge of Italian technology and terminology. The new type of crystal glass that the Bohemian glassworks were striving to produce, resulted in the end from a synthesis of the experience of various important glassworks. One of the very first enterprices of that kind was the Buquoy crystal glassworks in Nové Hrady, for the founding of which Louis Le Vasseur d'Ossimont of Arras was summoned. He came from the neighbourhood of the Buquoy estates near the Netherlands-French frontier, and he undoubtedly brought French glassmaking practice to Bohemia. On the other hand Michael Müller (1639—1709), master at the glassworks in the Vimperk region from 1671, based his work on the local tradition. He probably came from the Preussler works in Zejbiš in southern Bohemia. In 1683 he invented a way to perfect chalk glass, which then equalled crystal glass in quality. At the end of the 17th century he was the most famous master in Bohemia, and certainly greatly influenced the production of the glassworks in the Vimperk region.

In 1679 Bohuslav Balbín also speaks of shining crystal glass in his *Miscellanea regni Bohemiae,* in connection with other glassworks, such as that in Planá in the Plzeň region and one on the Counts of Kounic's estate in Nové Zámky. Crystal glass was also made in the Juliusthal glassworks on the Zákupy estate (Reichstadt) belonging to Duke Julius Francis of Saxony-Lauenburg (died 1689), which was also famous for its success in making ruby glass.

The quality of the engraved decorations on Bohemian glass improved sharply around 1700, when engraving in the new glass took on a more glyptic character. A new impetus that determined the appearance of Bohemian glass for the whole first half of the 18th century came about in 1710. At that time French decoration in the style of Jean Bérain spread throughout central Europe, making use of strapwork and garlands with grotesque elements, introduced by the prints of Paul Decker and other German engravers. The north Bohemian glass engravers got to know this type of ornament from the Meissen porcelain works, for which they cut and engraved Böttger's brown pottery from 1710 to 1713. This elegant decoration was used by the Bohemian engravers combined with coats-of-arms, portraits of rulers, figures of saints, allegorical figures of the Virtues and angels or with small hunting scenes, from the second decade of the 18th century up till around 1750.

The shapes of Bohemian glass too settled down during the first half of the 18th century into balanced proportions of several basic types of table glass—baluster goblets, little boat-shaped vessels for sweetmeats, conical beakers, flagons with tall necks. Only exceptionally some more articulated forms occur, such as beakers and sweetmeat bowls in the shape of a violin or octagonal goblets. An inseparable accompaniment to Bohemian glass of the 18th century is the facet cutting and printies. The preserved goblets and beakers are either individual pieces made as gifts or were part of travelling or table services.

The Česká Lípa region in northern Bohemia apart from being the most

71/ Goblet with plastic
volute and engraved
flowers,
Silesia, Petersdorf,
Friedrich Winter's
workshop, 1710—20

72/ Beaker, engraved in intaglio and relief, with putti on deer, Silesia, Petersdorf, Friedrich Winter, around 1700

important centre of refining glass, also grew into a centre of extensive, well organized trade in glass. It was the glass engravers themselves who were the first tradesmen. To start with they traded in a small way, setting out with bundles on their backs or pushing a barrow on long journeys lasting several months through Europe. Enterprising individuals, such as Georg Franz Kreybich, not only went to neighbouring Germany and Poland, but ventured as far as the Baltic countries, to Russia, Hungary, Transylvania, Wallachia and later too to France, Italy, Denmark, Sweden, England and Turkey. The most important market for Bohemian glass in the 18th century was Spain, from where Bohemian glass was then exported overseas. The successful merchants became wholesale traders in the 1720s and 1730s; they

73/ Beaker, engraved,
with allegorical figures of
the five senses after Martin
de Vos,
Silesia, around 1680

merged to form glass companies and founded their factories all along the coasts of Europe in thirty-eight ports, in twelve inland towns and outside Europe in Smyrna, Beirut, Cairo, Mexico, Baltimore and New York. So that during the first half of the 18th century Bohemian glass captured the world market.

In times of crisis and those of relative prosperity, dozens of glassmakers and engravers emigrated and spread abroad the style of Bohemian export glass, so that Bohemian decorative motifs can be seen, for instance, on glass from the Bohemian and Bavarian Forests, or in Thuringia, Poland, Russia and elsewhere.

Ornaments in the style of Jean Bérain were pleasing, in their classicism and balance, to other glass engravers as well, such as Anton Wilhelm Mäuerl of Nuremberg (1672—1737), one of the best engravers of the 18th century, who worked for the Nuremberg city patricians. Like the best Bohemian engravers, he introduced contrasts of dull and polished engraving into band and scroll ornament. Most of his preserved work is dated to the second decade of the 18th century. The same or perhaps even greater brilliance was achieved by Georg Ernst Kunckel (1692—1750), court engraver in Gotha in Thuringia. A large number of works are ascribed to him, mainly decorated with ornaments that originated in the 1720s and 1730s for Duke Frederick II of Saxony-Gotha.

French strapwork and scroll orna-

74/ Goblet, engraved, with small flower decoration and the coat-of-arms of Melchior Ducius von Wallenberg, castellan of Kynast, Silesia (Bohemian glass, Silesian engraving), around 1715

ments were special favourites in Saxony, which altogether followed French culture in many ways. The shapes of Saxon glass in the first third of the 18th century were very often close to the Bohemian ones, partly owing to the close relationship, already mentioned, between the glassmakers working in Bohemia and Saxony, and partly to the direct participation of Bohemian glassmakers in the production of glass in the most important Saxon glassworks, Neuostra, in the suburbs of Dresden, founded in 1699. Of course the "Königlich polnische kurfürstlich Sächsische Glashütte", which was intended to cater for the exacting demands of the Saxon court, sought for

75/ Covered goblet, engraved, with a view of Wrocław (Breslau) and a portrait of Frederick of Prussia in a medallion, Silesia, around 1750

[111

76/ Beaker, engraved, with a garden scene and the Schaffgotsch motto *Aucun temps ne me change,* Silesia, around 1720

eclectic inspiration from all sides. That is why shapes and manners of decoration appear among its products which come from the example of Potsdam glass or from Netherlands models, such as the flutes on champagne.

On the other hand, Bérain's type of decoration appears only exceptionally on Potsdam glass between 1708 and 1713, on goblets with the monograms of Friedrich I and his wives.

Silesian glass shows the strength of the tradition of the earlier ornaments, as opposed to the new ornamental models. Contemporary with Friedrich Winter's workshop, a number of engravers were active on the Schaffgotsch estates in the valley of Jelenia Góra (Hirschberg) at the end of the 17th century. Dense plant ornaments were characteristic of their work. At the beginning of the 18th century this orna-

[112

77/ Covered beaker, engraved, with a pastoral scene between an ornament of broad strapwork, Silesia, Warmbrunn, attributed to Christian Gottfried Schneider, around 1730—40

mentation became smaller and denser, and when around 1720 Bérain-type elements of strapwork and grotesques began to be incorporated it simply drowned in a confusion of tendrils and flower and leaf motifs. It was only designs of broad strapwork and lambrequins, widely used on Silesian glass from the end of the 1720s to the 1740s, that brought a new order to Silesian ornamention.

An entirely different style of engraved decoration developed where the engravers took as their model the monumental engraving of large crystal vessels. In Berlin the influence of work in crystal was shown in the use of relief cutting and in the more classical character in the use of the glyptic technique. Here large figured mythological scenes were used on glass, putti and heavy flowered valences, similar to

78/ Beaker, engraved, with the figure of a gentleman between Rococo ornaments, Silesia, Warmbrunn, attributed to Christian Gottfried Schneider, around 1750

German glass, 1st half of 18th century (1—3)

[114

German glass, 1st half
of 18th century

79/ Beaker, engraved,
with festoons of fruit,
Brandenburg, Potsdam,
Martin Winter's and
Gottfried Spiller's
workshop, around 1680

[115

those on ivory vessels and in goldsmiths' work in the second half of the
17th century. It is interesting how long
this style, intrinsically High Baroque,
lasted in Berlin. There is a reflection of
Spiller's mythological nudity in the
work of Elias Rosbach (1700–65),
who worked as an independent engraver in Berlin from 1727 to the 1740s,
on glass first from the Potsdam glassworks and, after this was closed, from
Zechlin. The same applies to a great
extent to Silesian engraving produced
by the followers of Friedrich Winter,
where figured motifs were used to
a much lesser extent. Here scenes with
putti predominate, after the prints by
Václav Hollar, and these, like Winter's
patterns of large flowers, continue on
Silesian glass till the end of the 1730s.
By that time, however, they were
linked with minutely engraved ornaments of broad strapwork.

On the other hand Franz Gondelach
in Cassel had no successor in his figured style. Johann Friedrich Trümper

80/ Covered goblet, engraved, with Bacchus on a barrel and a townscape, inscription *Ehrlich leben und fröhlich sein* ("Live honest and be happy"). Brandenburg, Potsdam, engraved in the style of Elias Rosbach, around 1725

81/ Goblet, engraved, with a river god in a landscape, inscription *Des Landes Wohlfahrt* ("Welfare of the country"), Brandenburg, Zechlin, Elias Rosbach, around 1740

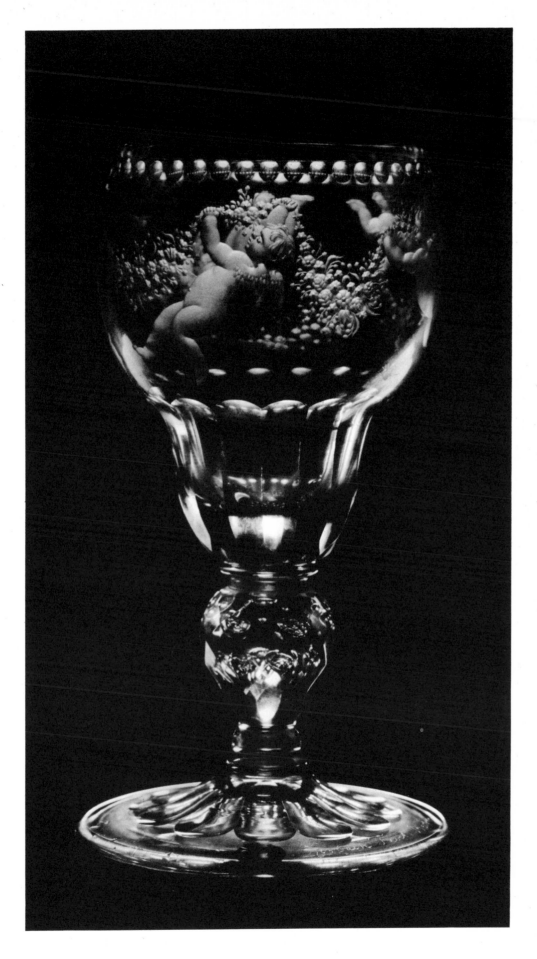

82/ Goblet, engraved, with putti and festoons, Brandenburg, Zechlin, Elias Rosbach, signed and dated 1740

[117

83/ Four-sided bottle,
engraved, with chinoiserie,
Nuremberg, Anton
Wilhelm Mäuerl, around
1720

84/ Covered goblet, engraved, with an allegorical figure of Justice, Nuremberg, Anton Wilhelm Mäuerl, around 1720

85/ Goblet, engraved, with the coat-of-arms of Friedrich II of Saxony-Gotha, Thuringia, Georg Ernst Kunckel, around 1720

of Cassel (died 1748), who was perhaps his pupil, took up quite a different style, close to that of the Silesian engravers. The nearest in style to Gondelach may have been Johann Moritz Trümper (died 1742), who left Cassel for Brandenburg in 1713 and there probably applied some of Gondelach's motifs on Potsdam glass.

No doubt the majority of engravers who cultivated the grand figured style of mythological scenes at the turn of the 17th and 18th centuries were always in some way connected with Berlin. This can also be said of the anonymous H. I., active from the end of the 17th century till about 1720, who is thought to have been Heinrich Jäger of Liberec. In Bohemia at first he worked on Potsdam glass and then in 1715—20 he is again found in Arnstad in Thuringia. Another engraver who

86/ Goblet, engraved, with a hunting scene, Thuringia, follower of Georg Ernst Kunckel, around 1720—30

also worked in Thuringia, Samuel Schwarz, originally from Gotha, cited in 1711 as the court engraver in Weissenfels, was undoubtedly influenced by the Berlin style. This is shown by the borders of Berlin type and the relief leaves on goblets that he supplied to various Thuringian courts until 1730. Also the work of Andreas Friedrich Sang (mentioned between 1719 and 1760) has links with the Berlin or Silesian figured style. He was born in Ilmenau in Thuringia, one of a large family of engravers who worked for Ernest August I of Saxony-Weimar.

In Dresden too large figured subjects occur between the years 1710 and 1730, evidently under the Potsdam influence. They are connected with the name of Johann Christoph Kiessling, who worked with his large workshop for the glass manufactory in 1717—44.

[121

87/ Beaker, engraved,
with Diana and Actaeon
between rocaille
ornaments,
Thuringia or Brunswick,
Johann Heinrich Balthasar
Sang, around 1745

88/ Flute, engraved, with
hunting scenes in medallions
between strapwork and
leaf tendril ornament,
Saxony, Dresden, around
1720

The works attributed to him include not only figured scenes, but virtuoso ornamental engraving, and also relief cut goblets in the Brandenburg style. This variety of styles can be partly explained by the fact that there were evidently engravers of varied training and origin in Kiessling's workshop. The last traces of relief cutting in Saxony are applied moulded relief portraits, used in the 1730s and 1740s.

Heinrich Friedrich Halter of Magdeburg may also, with certain reservations, be classified in the Potsdam circle. He worked from 1710 to 1720, engraving portraits and townscapes.

The great period of prosperity of Baroque engraved glass was at the end of the 17th century and the first half of the 18th. Later on the quality of the decoration rapidly declined. In Silesia, however, where engraved glass was made in the first place as gifts and souvenirs for the visitors to Cieplice spa (Warmbrunn), for the Leipzig Fairs or for personal or commercial friends, the standard of its decoration did not decline even in the middle of the 18th century, nor did the number of glass engravers. In 1742 there were forty-two of them in Warmbrunn alone and more came to the spa for the season to sell their goods. Around the middle of the 18th century Rococo ornaments appeared on Silesian glass, framing allegorical, gallant or working scenes, portraits, townscapes, chinoiserie etc. Many of these scenes were taken from the Augsburg engravings of J. W. Baumgartner, G. Hertel, E. Nilson and J. Rumpf, or from earlier engravings, such as the work of M. Küssel from the middle of the 17th century.

The most famous engraver of that time was Christian Gottfried Schneider (1710—73) of Warmbrunn, seventy paper prints of whose work have been preserved in Wrocław, showing the later style of his engraving. The only fully signed piece of Silesian Baroque glass is a goblet of the Merchants' Guild in Leipzig, now in the city museum there, which was made by Caspar Gottlieb Langer in 1749.

Another man who can also be considered an expressly Rococo glass engraver is the Thuringian, Johann Heinrich Balthasar Sang, son of Andreas Friedrich Sang, mentioned above, who worked until 1747 in Ilmenau and then became court glass engraver in Brunswick. A signed goblet in the Prague Decorative Arts Museum shows Sang's characteristic style, in which small mythological scenes are intermingled with rocaille ornaments.

Apart from the centres mentioned the production of engraved glass existed only in those places where it was introduced by migrating glass engravers, and in only few of those did it attain a high level. A number of preserved works show that an anonymous glass engraver, probably originally from Nuremberg, was active in the Netherlands as early as 1660—70. Then, after a long interval, further German engravers came to the Netherlands. Works from the first half of the 18th century, attributed to Christian Preussler, who settled in Amsterdam, are of Silesian character. In the second half of the 18th century it was mainly engravers of Thuringian origin who worked in the Netherlands, such as Jacob Sang (died 1783) and Simon Jacob Sang, no doubt relations. Both of them show a certain influence of An-

Hessen glass, 18th century, under English influence (1—4)

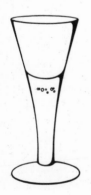

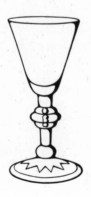

dreas Friedrich Sang of Ilmenau, whom we find in Amsterdam in 1748. In the case of Christian and Christoffel Grisnicht Schröder, on the other hand, there is evident influence of the Berlin school of Elias Rosbach. W. O. Robart (1696—1778), who worked in The Hague, was of Dutch origin. The majority of these engravers, like the makers of stippled decorations, used English glass. Heinrich Gottlieb Köhler, who worked for the Saxon Glass Company in Copenhagen until 1746, where he was court glass engraver, shows in style his Silesian origin. From the end of the 1750s he worked in Nøstetangen in Norway and eventually founded his own glassworks in Christiania. A number of unimportant Bohemian and German engravers worked in Sweden too, as they did in Poland, where engraved glass strongly influenced by Saxony and Bohemia originated. Saxon influences are also evident in Russian cut and engraved glass of the 18th century, simply decorated

91/ Goblet, engraved,
with a bacchanal,
Saxony, Dresden, around
1720

92/ Goblet, engraved, with a bust of Maria Theresia and cross faceting, Saxony, around 1745

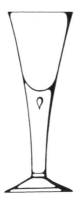

English glass, 18th century (1—8)

Goblet with lid, engraved, with the monogram of Charles XII (1697—1718), Sweden, Kungsholm Glasbruck, around 1715

portraits of rulers with undemanding ornaments. The engraved decorations of glass made in the second half of the 18th century by a glassworks in La Granja de San Ildefonso in Castile are of a very low standard.

Some English engraved glass of the 18th century reflects the struggle between the Stuarts and the House of Orange. What are known as Jacobite goblets were made for toasts to the Stuarts, with portraits of James Edward and Charles Edward (the Old and Young Pretenders) and with symbols of a rose and a rosebud and inscriptions such as "Fiat" ("Let it be done"), "Redeat" ("May he return"), "Audentior ibo" ("I will go more boldly") (up till 1745). Disguised Jacobite symbols then occur till 1770, when the Stuart cause was lost, and after that more openly as a commemoration. However, there also exist symbols and inscriptions expressing sympathy for the ruling House of Orange, with motifs of orange trees and inscriptions celebrating the battles won. In comparison with the central European production, however, the quality of the English engraved glass at this time is only very average.

Advice to Collectors and Recommended Literature

Baroque engraved glass forms an extensive chapter in the history of European glassmaking. A basic classification of this material was made by R. Schmidt in *Brandenburgische Gläser,* Berlin 1914, *Die Gläser der Sammlung Mühsam,* Berlin 1914, *Das Glas,* Berlin 1922, *Die Gläser der Sammlung Mühsam, Neue Folge,* Berlin 1926, and in various publications by G. E. Pazaurek. The biggest post-war book on the subject is by E. Meyer-Heisig, *Der Nürnberg Glasschnitt des 17. Jahrhunderts,* Nuremberg 1963, on the Nuremberg engravers of the 17th century. The same author also dealt with the personality of C. Lehmann: "Caspar Lehmann. Ein Beitrag zur Frühgeschichte des deutschen Glasschnittes", *Anzeiger des Germanischen Nationalmuseums 1963, Festschrift Ludwig Grote,* pp. 116 ff, based on an earlier work: W. Holzhausen, "Dresden-Prager Glas- und Steinschnitt um 1600", *Neues Archiv für sächsische Geschichte und Altertumskunde,* Dresden 1934.

O. Drahotová writes on Bohemian engraved glass: "Dans la sphère du maître graveur du goblet dit de Koula", *Cristal de Bohême* 1964, pp. 29—32, "Glas aus Venedig oder Sachsen. Ein Beitrag zur Frage des Venezianischen Glases in böhmischer Art", *Jahrbuch der Staatlichen Kunstsammlungen Dresden* 1965/6, pp. 153—160, "Bohemian Glassdécor in the Style of Jean Bérain", *Annales* 1967, "Bohemian Crystal Glass and its Imitation in Venice in the 18th Century", *Annales* 1970, "Medals and Coins as Designs for Engraved Baroque Glass in the Museum of Decorative Arts in Prague", *Czechoslovak Glass Review* 7, 1972, pp. 29—32, "North Bohemian Engraved Baroque Glass as One of Historically Located Relics", *Ars Vitraria* 4, 1973, pp. 20—35, 127—128. The latest publications on Saxon glass were written by G. Haase, *Sächsisches Glas vom 17. bis zum Anfang des 19. Jahrhunderts,* Staatliche Kunstsammlungen Dresden. Ausstellung des Museums für Kunsthandwerk, Schloss Pillnitz, Dresden 1975, S. Baumgärtner, *Sächsisches Glas, Die Glashütten und ihre Erzeugnisse,* Wiesbaden 1977. Thuringian glass is dealt with by A. Janda, "Der Thüringische Glasschnitt im 17. Jahrhundert", Phil. diss., Universität Leipzig, Ms. 1962, R. J. Charleston, "The Monogramist 'HI', a Notable German Engraver", *JGS* IV, 1962, pp. 67—84, and J. C. Roselt, "Samuel Schwarz, Glasschnitt-Meister in Thüringen", *JGS* IV, 1962, pp. 85—102. The basic handbook on Silesian glass is by E. von Czihak, *Schlesische Gläser, eine Studie über die Schlesische Glasindustrie früherer Zeit nebst einem beschreibenden Katalog der Gläsersammlung des Museums Schlesischer Altertümer zu Breslau,* Wrocław 1891. Further historical information on engraved glass is given by H. Seydel, *Beiträge zur Geschichte des Siegelstein- und Glasschnitts und der Glaserzeugung im Riesen- und Isergebirge, Schlesiens Vorzeit in Bild und Schrift,* Wrocław 1919. Newer articles on the history of Silesian glass have been published by A. Chrzanowska, "Odbitki dekoracij szkiel Christiana Gottfrieda Schneidera", *Roczniki Sztuki Slaskiej* II, Wrocław 1963, pp. 128—132, and F. A. Dreier, "Stichvorlagen und Zeichnungen zu

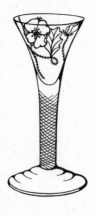

Goblet, engraved, with the Jacobite rose, England, around 1750

93/ Funnel-shaped goblet,
engraved, with
a townscape,
Hessen, around 1750

94/ Goblet, engraved,
with a coat-of-arms,
Hessen or Lauenstein,
around 1760—70

95/ Goblet, engraved, with a portrait of Charles XII of Sweden and a view of the Battle of Narva, Sweden, dated 1700

96/ Goblet, engraved, with a bust of Russian Czarina Elizabeth Petrovna (1745—62), Russia, around 1750

Gläsern Christian Gottfried Schneiders", *JGS* VII, 1965, pp. 66—78, who has also written a new book on Hessen glass, *Glaskunst in Hessen und Kassel*, Cassel 1969. Baroque engraved glass is constantly followed by B. Klesse, *Glassammlung Helfried Krug*, vol. I, Munich 1965, "Allegorische und mythologische Kupferstichvorlagen im Glasschnitt des Barock", *JGS* XIV, 1972, pp. 117—140, *Glassammlung Helfried Krug*, vol. II, Bonn 1973, *500 Jahre Glaskunst, Sammlung Biemann*, Rastatt 1978. H. E. Gelder writes about glass engravers in the Netherlands: "Achttiende-eeuwse glas-snijders in Holland", *Oud Holland* LXXIII, 1958, pp. 1—17, 90—102, 148—155, 211—219. For the history of technology of cutting and engraving glass see R. J. Charleston, "Wheel-engraving and Cutting, Some Early Equipment. I. Engraving", *JGS* 1964;

II. "Water-power and Cutting", *JGS* 1965, who also wrote about G. Ravenscroft, "George Ravenscroft: New Light on the Development of his Cristaline Glasses", *JGS* 1968. H. Seitz writes about the work of engravers in the north of Europe, *Äldre svenska glas med graverad dekor*, Stockholm 1936, and so does A. Polak, "Nøstetangen, Köhler og Schlesien", *Yearbook*, Kunstindustrimuseet, Oslo 1966. Engraved glass was most copied in northern Bohemia in the regions of Kamenický Šenov and Mistrovice, often under contract for the firm of J. & L. Lobmeyr. Also the firm of Meyr's Neffe at Adolfov produced good copies of Bohemian and Silesian glass around 1900. In Wrocław (Breslau) the firm of Moritz Wentzel made copies of Silesian glass at the beginning of the 20th century. All these three firms usually signed their products.

Bohemian glass, 2nd half of 18th century: drawings from sample list of Harrach glassworks in Nový Svět (1—11)

[133

Glass Painted with Schwarzlot of the 17th and 18th Centuries

Schwarzlot (literally "black lead") is a glassmaker's enamel paint. Fired linear grisaille painting with Schwarzlot can be found in medieval stained glass windows and in Swiss and south German panes from the 16th and 17th centuries, painted with transparent enamels. A later painter of window panes, Johann Schaper (1621—70), who worked in Nuremberg from 1655, transferred the technique to hollow glass and faience. He was probably influenced by the Dutch Schwarzlot landscape paintings on gold foil, which he may have seen in northern Germany, where he was born and served his apprenticeship. The earliest of Schaper's black painted glass is dated around 1660, the last 1667. Many pieces are signed with his monogram or his whole name. His landscapes with ruins, portraits and battle scenes are carefully painted and have details scratched in with a needle. Some rare specimens have been preserved of his work with transparent enamels and paintings on faience.

The first of Schaper's Nuremberg followers were also qualified painters of glass windows and also worked both on faience and glass. From the 1670s we know the work of Johann Keyll, Hermann Bencherlt and a man who used the monogram G. H. The younger generation of painters included Johann Ludwig Faber (mentioned 1678—97), who is also known from faience paintings. Abraham Helmhack (1654—1724) too, though he was a qualified glass painter, only left us painted faience vessels. All these Nuremberg artists were Hausmaler (freelance painters), independent of any glassworks or faience manufactory. We can also count amongst them Georg Strauch, who painted both glass and faience in opaque enamel paints.

The tradition of the Hausmaler continued in the 18th century too in the decoration of porcelain. Then Nuremberg ceased to be the main centre of Hausmalerei, which moved instead to Augsburg, Bohemia, Silesia and Vienna. In Bohemia and Silesia the big name in Hausmalerei is that of the Preissler family. On the Rychnov estates, in Kunštát (Kronstadt), which belonged to Count Franz Karl Liebsteinsky von Kolowrat, we know of Daniel Preissler (died 1733) and his son Ignatius (1676—1741). Both worked for their lord on both glass and porcelain. Before he came to Kunštát in 1680 Daniel Preissler was a glasspainter in Bedřichov (Friedrichswald), which was right on the Bohemian-Silesian border. Some uncertainty about the attribution of glass painted in Preissler's style has been caused by a glasspainter named Preissler, who worked in Wrocław, being mentioned in 1723 by a Wrocław doctor and art expert J. C. Kundmann. We do not know which member of the family this refers to. But there does exist a black painted goblet with the Wrocław coat-of-arms, now in the Strasser collection in New York, where the work of Ignatius Preissler is also kept, that comes from the Kolowrat property. The published accounts of Ignatius Preissler from 1729 to 1739 help to identify him as a painter of chinoiserie decoration, but also of glass with demanding themes or "poetic laborious objects". Preissler's strapwork and scroll ornaments and grotesque motifs show a close relationship with the decoration of early Viennese porcelain of the Du Paquier period. Both Preisslers complemented their black paintings with steel-point scratching and painting in gold.

97/ Covered beaker painted in Schwarzlot, with the bust of a man in a medallion and landscape, Nuremberg, Johann Schaper, dated 1666

[135

98/ Beaker painted in
Schwarzlot, with a lion
hunt, after A. Tempesta,
Nuremburg, monogramist
H.G., dated 1673

99/ Covered goblet
painted in Schwarzlot, with
an allegory of Abundantia,
eastern Bohemia,
Kunštát, Ignaz Preissler,
around 1730

100/ Bowl painted in Schwarzlot with the Kolowrat coat-of-arms and grotesque ornament, eastern Bohemia, Kunštát, Ignaz Preissler, around 1725

Advice to Collectors and Recommended Literature

Nuremberg glass painted with Schwarzlot by Hausmaler still needs thorough research. After R. Schmidt (*Das Glas,* Berlin 1922) it has been extensively written about only by G. E. Pazaurek (*Deutsche Fayence- und Porzellan-Hausmaler,* Leipzig 1925). The Bohemian glass of Ignatius Preissler was first identified by F. X. Jiřík in *Ignác Preissler, Zprávy kuratoria Uměleckoprůmyslového muzea v Praze* (Report of the Curatorium of the Museum of Decorative Arts in Prague),

Prague 1924; *České sklo* (Bohemian Glass), Prague 1934. A later publication on glass from the Kolowrat property is by R. von Strasser, "Twelve Preissler Glasses", *JGS* XV, 1973, pp. 135 ff. A collected edition on the Nuremberg home painters is being prepared by H. Bosch (Munich).
Copies of this type of glass occur rather rarely. In Bohemia Preissler's style was imitated by the firm of Meyr's Neffe at Adolfov around 1890.

Zwischengoldglas of the 18th Century

Baroque double-walled glass is a development of an idea published in 1679 by Johann Kunckel in the first edition of *Ars Vitraria Experimentalis*. The principle of this form of decoration is the use of two vessels made so that they fit precisely into one another. The inner vessel is decorated on its outer side with gold or silver leaf, and this is protected by the outer covering. This technique continues a tradition already known in ancient times. In Kunckel's method the gold is not glassed over under heat, but the two vessels are joined cold with a resinous varnish. A Baroque feature here is the idea of imitation semi-precious stones with marbled oil painting. Some goblets of this kind do exist and they are traditionally attributed to Kunckel, but their size, shape, type of glass and manner of faceting show their Bohemian origin. The great majority of Baroque double-walled glasses and vases originated in Bohemia, the themes of their decoration being connected with Czech saints, localities, Church dignitaries and nobles. The principle of production, in contrast to Kunckel's prescription, was an improved placing of the upper seam, in which the join between the two glasses is apparent, below the upper edge of the vessel, and the fitting of the bottomless outer vessel with a glass disc which is finally stuck in place underneath with a resinous varnish. The decoration with oil colours was omitted and gold leaf used instead, allowing graphic decoration.

Thick-walled beakers belong to the older type of Bohemian Zwischengoldglas, which are cut into broad facets that reflect the double-walled medallion on the bottom. Engraved pieces of similar shape are dated to between 1710 and 1715. Probably still older are two double-walled plates, kept in Prague and Liberec, painted with red transparent varnish and decorated with scrolls and the coats-of-arms of Mathias Desfours and Polyxena Hartmann of Klarstein, with engraved gold leaf; according to the dates of the wedding and death of Mathias Desfours,

they probably originated between 1698 and 1710. Close to these in decoration are beakers entirely painted with red varnish and decorated either with vertically cut garlands in gold or silver leaf, placed across the facets of the beakers, or big acanthus leaves covering the whole surface.

Some time ago attempts were made to classify these products in the history of Bohemian glass. In the older literature there were two hypotheses concerning the origin of these glasses: that Zwischengoldglas originated in the monasteries and that it was made in the Harrach glassworks in Nový Svĕt. More recent research has tried to give a clue to the solution of this question in the figure of Father Pacificus Kligel (Kliegel, died 1746), whose name is engraved on a beaker with the fourteen Stations of the Cross, last seen at an auction sale in Cologne in 1894 by G. E. Pazaurek. Father Kligel did in fact preach in the Franciscan monastery in Hejnice in northern Bohemia, and also in Hostinné and Silesia. As a member of the order of Franciscan Mendicant Friars, Kligel went round the important glassmaking areas around Nový Svĕt, Jablonec and Česká Lípa twice a year, and he also visited the Sporck estates in Kuks, so that all the places where Zwischengoldglas is supposed to have been made are connected with his name.

According to material that has been preserved it is clear that a small workshop produced double-walled vessels throughout the first half of the 18th century. Later work, from the second quarter of the 18th century, is distinguished from the earlier products by a wider knowledge of the ornamental and figured graphic models. This group includes, besides religious and hunting subjects, scenes from the life of the nobles, which lead to the supposition that one of the engravers may have had connections with the circle around Count Sporck, who led a high-level social life in Kuks, where he founded a spa and held concerts, theatrical productions and, of course, large hunting expeditions. Other work, decorated with views of Hejnice monastery, can, with some hesitation, be attributed to Pacificus Kligel, so long, of course, as he was the maker and not the owner to whom the lost beaker was given.

Extensive production of Zwischengoldglas ended some time after the middle of the 18th century. In the 1740s we often find double-walled glasses painted with coloured transparent varnishes. It seems that double-walled glass was produced in small quantities even in the second half of the 18th century. A special group, the style of which covers the whole first half of the 18th century, consists of works decorated with double-walled medallions; they are for the most part the remains of large table services, also decorated with facet cutting and engraved ornaments. One such complete service has been preserved in Baden, where it was ordered by the Margravine Sibylla Augusta (wife of Ludwig of Baden), who came from Bohemia.

There is a small group of beakers, goblets and plates that is different in shape technique from typical Bohemian work, but is decorated with gold leaf and opaque dark varnishes, sometimes also marbled. These beakers are of unusual shape—bell-like and rounded at the bottom. The goblet is most reminiscent of Saxon glass. The gold leaf is mostly confined to the ornamental border and a single figured motif or a butterfly on the surface. Judging from the decoration and the inscription on the plate referring to the Battle of Chotusitz (1742), these specimens can be dated to the 1730s and 1740s. They are mostly considered to be of Saxon make.

The work of Johann Sigismund Menzel (1744—1810) is clearly influenced by Bohemian Zwischengoldglas of the first half of the 18th century. He decorated glass with double-walled medallions bearing silhouette portraits of the spa visitors in Warmbrunn. His work, carried out on Silesian glass of classical shapes, is only a little earlier than that of Johann Joseph Mildner (1763—1808), who worked in Guttenbrunn, on the estates of the Counts of Fürnberg in Austria. Some two hundred pieces of his work have been preserved, most of them signed and dated between 1787 and 1807. The double-walled pieces are mostly confined to medallions on the walls, sometimes on the bottom, and to ornamental friezes on the edge. Very rarely do we find a beaker that is entirely double-walled. The medallions are usually decorated with monograms, coats-of-arms, portraits of Count Fürnberg, views of the castle and buildings in the locality of Guttenbrunn or figures of saints.

Advice to Collectors and Recommended Literature

Knowledge on double-walled glass was first collected by G. E. Pazaurek, "Die Heimat der Zwischengoldgläser", *Mitteilungen des Nordböhmischen Gewerbe-Museums* 1898, XVL, pp. 53; *Die Gläsersammlung des Nordböhmischen Gewerbemuseums in Reichenberg*, Leipzig 1902, and later by R. Schmidt, *Das Glas*, Berlin 1912, 2nd edition, 1922; *Die Gläser der Sammlung Mühsam*, Berlin 1914, and F. K. Jiřík, "Klenoty sklářské" (Glass Gems), *Zlatá Praha* (Golden Prague) 1914, XXXI, pp. 31; *České sklo* (Bohemian Glass), Prague 1934. At present J. Brožová is most advanced in research in this branch: "České dvojstěnné sklo a jeho autoři" (Bohemian Double-walled Glass and Its Masters), *Acta UPM* (Decorative Arts Museum) VII, Prague 1973, and she is preparing a scientific catalogue of the big collection of double-walled glass in the Decorative Arts Museum in Prague. Questions of double-walled glass of Saxon origin have been collected by A. von Saldern, "Zwischengoldgläser mit marmorierter Lackbemalung", *Anzeiger des Germanischen Nationalmuseums* 1976, pp. 133—142. G. E. Pazaurek deals with the work of Menzel and J. J. Mildner, "Die Gläser der Warmbrunner Menzel-Werkstadt und J. J. Mildner", *Belvedere* 8, 1925, pp 57—70.

Zwischengoldglas was often falsified at the end of the 19th century and in the 20th. The technique of its production was mastered by F. Schreiber in Volary (Wallern, 1878—1944), who also imitated J. J. Mildner. Between the two world wars double-walled glass was also imitated in north Bohemia in the Kamenický Šenov region. Forgeries of double-walled glass vessels can usually be recognized by the technique of their production and the style of their engravings. Recently the technology of sandwich glass was dealt with by L. Neustifter in *Die Weltkunst* 1978, pp. 320—323, 742—745, 1156—1159, and by R. Brill, C. A. Aiken, D. T. Novick, R. F. Errest, "Conservation Problems of Zwischengold Glass, Part I. Examinations and Analyses", *JGS* XXII, Corning 1980, pp. 12—35.

Ruby Glass and Coloured Glass of the 17th and 18th Centuries

The advance of glassmaking north of the Alps in the second half of the 17th century brought with it an interest in coloured glass. The leading glassworks in central Europe, such as the Potsdam glassworks and the Saxon Heidelbach glassworks in the Ore Mountains, revived production of blue glass coloured with cobalt, previously produced here at the turn of the 16th and 17th centuries. We also find white, manganese violet and dark green glass. All these colour tones were used throughout the 17th century in Italy and in the Netherlands, and a knowledge of their production technique probably spread from there. The popularity of opal glass, which the Murano and French glassmakers had started making after the middle of the 17th century, reached to Germany and Bohemia in the 1670s. Some colour tones, especially cobalt blue, manganese violet and honey yellow, caught on in the Bavarian and Tyrol regions, where optically decorated bottles for spirits were made from coloured glass for the broad mass of the people from the end of the 17th century.

The production of these kinds of coloured glass was based on earlier traditions and knowledge, whereas the mysterious ruby glass, coloured with gold, is the fruit of 17th-century alchemy. Its beginnings are connected with the name of the chemist and alchemist Johann Kunckel (about 1630—1703). Kunckel made experiments with the production of ruby glass some time before 1679, when he mentions it in the first edition of *Ars Vitraria*. He was then working for the Brandenburg Elector Friedrich Wilhelm (died 1688) in the Drewitz glassworks near Potsdam, and from 1679 in the new glassworks at the edge of the town. Kunckel made use of old experience in his experiments. The colouring properties of gold are mentioned by Georg Agricola as far back as 1546 in his book *De natura fossilium,* and also in 1612 by Antonio Neri. Kunckel made use of experiments by the Hamburg doctor Andreas Cassius, who succeeded in making what was called "purple of Cassius", though not in his attempts to colour molten glass permanently. Kunckel worked with gold precipitated with tin (precipitatio Solis cum Iove). For ruby glass he used pure gold, dissolved in aqua regia (one part nitric acid, three parts hydrochloric acid), to make gold chloride, also used by Cassius. The red colouring of the glass was caused by the scattered submicroscopic particles of gold. The fired glass had to be reheated for the colour to appear. Colouring glass red with copper had been known since ancient times, but the gold-dyed ruby glass had a special value, given not only by the more beautiful tone of the colour, but also by the magical effects ascribed to it, as to real jewels. The production of gold ruby glass in Potsdam evidently continued after Kunckel's departure, and his recipe was also known in the later Brandenburg glassworks at Zechlin.

The making of gold ruby glass did not remain Kunckel's secret for long. According to Kunckel himself, the "modus procedendi" was betrayed to the Duke of Saxony-Lauenburg to Ostrov (Schlackenwerth) in Bohemia by Kunckel's own Christallmeister. Another of Kunckel's servants is said to have sold the secret of ruby glass to the Bayreuth court and elsewhere. We know from other sources that ruby glass was made in Freysing at the end of the 17th century and that in 1690 it was made in Munich by Hans Christoph Fiedler for the Bavarian Elector Max Emmanuel. The same Fiedler temporarily headed the Juliusthal glassworks on the Zákupy estates (Reichstadt) in 1687/8, which was owned, together with the Ostrov estates, by Duke Julius Francis of Saxony-Lauenburg (died 1689). Here he not only produced crystal glass, but also experimented with ruby glass. The ruby glass in Baden, where the Duke's daughter Sibylla Augusta became the wife of the

Margrave of Baden, and documents in the archives on the division of the legacies, prove that the experiments in the Juliusthal glassworks were successful, even though production was evidently never very big.

In old Bohemian sources Michael Müller (died 1709), mentioned above, is given as the first maker of ruby glass in Bohemia, and he also made glass striped with ruby and gold, that is with a ruby thread decoration, later used in the stems of Bohemian Baroque goblets. Christian Preussler's glassworks in Schreiberhau in Silesia is also mentioned to have known the technique of making ruby glass. It is clear that both the Bohemian and Silesian production of Baroque ruby glass was very restricted, and so only very few preserved specimens exist. They are mostly lighter in colour than the glass made by Kunckel and facet cutting is a typical feature.

The south German production, probably in Munich, was much more extensive at the end of the 17th century and beginning of the 18th. It includes decoratively ribbed bottles, vases, goblets, beakers and caskets mounted in gold, most often with the Augsburg goldsmiths' marks. Besides these elaborate objects, pharmaceutical bottles were made in south Germany, often sets of them in small boxes.

Ruby glass of Saxon origin shows a different technical procedure, ascribed to J. F. Böttger. As distinct from other contemporary products, this is layered glass. Some examples of this production, dated to between 1713 and 1718, have been preserved in the collections of the Grünes Gewölbe in Dresden. Besides other things, they are a precious testimony to the knowledge of making layered glass at the beginning of the 18th century.

Quite different again in character was the transparent red glass made by Bernard Perrot in Orléans. According to analysis this too was based on the colouring effects of gold, but was evidently connected with Perrot's making of imitation jewels. The ruby threaded Bohemian Baroque glass probably comes from this French source rather than from Kunckel's gold ruby glass.

It is interesting to compare the engraved decorations on ruby glass. Some few Potsdam pieces were decorated with figured engraving of Spiller's type. The south German glass is usually engraved with a simple flower and leaf ornament of acanthus leaves and putti, festoons or landscapes. Some of these decorated works of no great quality have been attributed, probably wrongly, to Johann Heel (died 1709), a Nuremberg faience painter, or the contemporary Nuremberg engraver Paulus Eder (died 1709). But there also exists ruby glass engraved by the good Nuremberg engravers, such as G. F. Killinger (died 1726).

Advice to Collectors and Recommended Literature

Potsdam ruby glass has been dealt with by R. Schmidt, *Brandenburgische Gläser*, Berlin 1914; *Die Gläser der Sammlung Mühsam*, Berlin 1926. In the 1930s a number of articles were published, giving details of Kunckel as a personality and the production technology of ruby glass: H. Maurach, "Johann Kunckel", *Deutsches Museum, Abhandlungen und Berichte* 5, no. 2, 1933; W. Ganzenmüller, "Beiträge zur Geschichte des Goldrubinglases", parts I, II, III, *Glastechnische Berichte* 15, Sept. 1937, no. 9, p. 346 ff.; October 1937, p. 379 ff.; November 1937, p. 417 ff.; W. Holzhausen, "Sächsiches Rubinglas Steingefässe von J.F. Böttger", *Belvedere* 12, 1934, pp. 16–22, deals with J. F. Böttger's Dresden glass. R. Berliner, "Eine Münchner Glashütte im letzten Viertel des 17. Jahrhunderts", *Münchner Jahrbuch für bildende Kunst*, NF I, 1924, pp. 109 ff., gives information on the making of ruby glass in Munich. Since the war this theme has been written on by Franz-Adrian Dreier, "Kunst- gewerbemuseum — Neuerwerbungen und Schenkungen 1971", *Jahrbuch Preussischer Kulturbesitz* IX, 1971, pp. 257–264, O. Drahotová, "Das böhmische Rubinglas an der Wende des 17. und 18. Jahrhunderts", *Glasrevue* No. 4, Prague 1973, J. Fetzer, *Johann Kunckel, Leben und Werk eines grossen deutschen Glasmachers des 17. Jahrhundert*, Berlin 1977, and R. J. Charleston, *The James A. de Rothschild Collection at Waddesdon Manor, Glass and Enamels*, London 1977. Most of the ruby glass to be found in collections and on the antiques market is probably of south German origin. There are also quite a number of imitations from the 19th and 20th centuries. We know, for instance, that the so-called Kunckelrubin coloured with gold was made in the glassworks in Nový Svět (Neuwelt) in northern Bohemia in the 1840s. Most later imitations are coloured with copper, layered or merely ruby stained.

101/ Goblet, engraved, with allegorical figures of War and Peace, Nuremberg, attributed to Hermann Schwinger, around 1670—80

102/ Covered goblet, engraved, with figures of the Emperor and the Turkish Sultan on Horseback, northern Bohemia, probably the Jablonec region, around 1730

103/   Ruby glass and ruby
threaded glass, cut faceting,
Bohemia, around 1690

104/ Ruby glass, optically
ribbed and engraved, in
gilded mounts,
southern Germany, around
1700

105/ Beaker,
double-walled, decorated
with engraved flowers in
gold leaf and red
transparent varnish,
Bohemia, around 1710

[149

106/ Goblet,
double-walled, decorated
with engraving of a riding
school scene in gold leaf,
Bohemia, around 1720—25

107/ Detail of transparently painted double-walled goblet, Bohemia, around 1745

Imitation Porcelain of the Second Half of the 18th Century

In the history of industrial arts oriental porcelain has often been a source of inspiration and object of imitation. Some of these imitations are faience and soft-paste porcelain, while some are opaque white glass. The term "porcellana contrafatta" has been used in Venice since 1504.

From the beginning of the 17th century the Dutch East India Company arranged the regular import of oriental goods, Chinese porcelain among other things, and this further encouraged efforts to imitate it, both in ceramics and in glass. The attempts to imitate porcelain in glass were mostly made in the third quarter of the 17th century, and they are interwoven with the production of opal glass of a similar composition.

In 1669 "porcelain made of glass" was produced with ingredients of lead, tin and bone ash, by Joachim Becher, court doctor and alchemist to the Bavarian Elector Ferdinand Maria in Munich. In 1679 Johann Kunckel published a recipe for making opal glass, and he also actually made it, as is confirmed by the Silesian author Johann Christian Kundmann in 1737. Yet we do not know of any surviving results of this production.

In the 1670s opal glass became extremely popular. It was made not only in Venice, but also in France, where its production is linked with the name of the well-known glassmaker Bernard Perrot. There is a story that in 1686 Madame Perrot accompanied the Siamese ambassador through the glassworks and showed him the perfect imitations of oriental porcelain, enamels, crystal, agate and opal glass, lapis lazuli or ruby in colour, and finally imitations of many precious stones. This is why figured table ornaments of white opaque glass on transparent pedestals with ruby dots in the pincered details are attributed to Bernard Perrot. In 1686 Perrot's rival, Nicolas Massolay (of the Venetian family of Mazzolà) was also granted a patent to make im-

Flacon with a rounded stopper, opaque-white glass, enamel-painted, France, around 1715—20

108/ Mug of milk glass, enamel-painted, with allegorical figure of Africa, Bohemia, Nový Svět, around 1770

itation porcelain, and he also made opaque white glass in Orléans and later in Paris and Rouen until 1729. During the whole of the first third of the 18th century white wedding cups with quasi-folk enamel painted decorations were produced, mainly in Normandy and Lorraine. At the same time painted milk glass was being made, decorated with motifs of palm-leaf fans, which may have come from Nicolas Massolay's glassworks. The production of opal and milk glass in the south Bohemian glassworks in the 1670s and 1680s was based on French ideas.

There are several different recipes for making milk glass. Different regions made it differently: Venetian production gave priority to opacifying it with tin and lead in the presence of chalk, we know that Bernard Perrot coloured his glass with antimony, other French recipes call for a mixture of arsenic, and Kunckel advises the use of bone and horn ash. This last method leads to a transparent opal glass with orange effects. The whole German production of 18th-century milk glass, which is never entirely opaque, is based on Kunckel. Even Bohemian recipes of the beginning of the 19th century still recommend a mixture of bone ash and not of tin.

Even though all these productions are conscious imitations of porcelain, they did not attempt to make a faithful copy of it either in shape or decoration. This tendency only became evident in the 18th century. Venetian painted milk glass of the beginning of the 18th century imitates majolica from Castelli, decorated with landscape motifs and Venetian Vezzi porcelain with chinoiserie. Pieces from the Miottis' "Al Gesù" workshop of around 1740, with painted flowers or views of Venice, are even more like porcelain.

It is difficult to classify the production of little cups and bowls, of slightly transparent glass, decorated with manganese or cobalt blue spots and in form based directly on models of Chinese porcelain. They may be of Venetian, French or German origin. There is a continuation of them in little cups, deep bowls, pots and mugs, most of them dating to the 1740s, which are derived from the shape and decoration of the blue painted Chinese export porcelain of the turn of the 17th and 18th centuries. They can be distinguished by rather poor quality painting of chinoiserie and quasi-oriental friezes with white blanks and diagonal lines. They are perhaps of Thuringian origin, possibly coming from glassworks in Lauscha. It is interesting to note their similarity in motif to contemporary faience in Bayreuth.

Bohemian milk glass began to flourish after 1764, when the Harrach glassworks in Nový Svět (Neuwelt) started making it. Production soon grew rapidly and it won success on markets both at home and abroad. Fig-

ured Rococo painting was widely used on Harrach glass, imitating the decoration of German Rococo porcelain. Most often this consists of love and hunting scenes with indications of landscapes and little buildings, passing into rocaille and combing. François Boucher's influence can be seen, as interpreted in the engravings of Chodowiecki, Nilson and others. But no actual models have so far been found. There is no lack of religious themes from the Old and New Testament and figures of the saints, based on holy pictures. There is also a wide range of allegories, starting with Church allegories such as the Christian Virtues, then allegories of the times of day, the months, the elements and continents, models for which could be found in late editions of Ripa's *Iconography*. From the 1780s onwards there are more figures in semi-classical medal-

109/ Cup and saucer of milk glass, enamel-painted, with motifs from oriental porcelain, Thuringia, around 1745—50

110/ Vase and inkwell of milk glass painted with enamel,
northern Bohemia, Bor region, 3rd quarter of 18th century

Covered sugar bowl of milk glass, ribbed, with enamel painted flowers, Bohemia, Nový Svět, 1780s

Little jug of milk glass with enamel-painted flowers, Bohemia, Nový Svět, around 1790

lions, evidently taken from fashion magazines of the period. Very often there appear flower motifs in rosy hues. At this time whole services were made of milk glass, imitating contemporary porcelain in shape so far as possible.

English milk glass (generally called "opaque white glass") of the second half of the 18th century has its own specific character. This comes in the first place from its close relationship to contemporary English porcelain. At one time the milk glass made in Bristol won great fame — which is why the majority of English milk glass that has been preserved is supposed to have come from there. According to the newest ideas, based on the relationship between English opaque white glass and the porcelain products from Worcester and also the glazed pottery from Staffordshire, it is more likely that most of the "Bristol ware" actually came from glassworks in the Midlands. Therefore many of these products cannot be attributed to Michael Edkins (1734—1811), who worked in Bristol, as is traditionally done in older English literature. As compared with Bohemian glass, the substance of the English milk glass is much more opaque and the painting finer, with more expressly

[155

Neo-classical features which appear in England much earlier than on the continent. The same can be said of gold painting, which was done by James Giles (1718—80), who worked in London. Giles decorated English porcelain in his workshop, and also opaque white, blue and green glass, with figures of country people, birds and flowers in the Neo-classical style.

Advice to Collectors and Recommended Literature

The milk glass of the 17th and 18th centuries is another chapter that has been little researched. There is information on French production in an article by J. Barrelet, "Porcelaines de verre en France", *Cahiers de la Céramique et des Arts du Feu* XXXVI, Paris 1965, p. 254 ff. English milk glass is dealt with by R. J. Charleston, "Michael Edkins and the Problem of English Enamelled Glass", *Transactions of the Society of Glass Technology,* 1954; "English Opaque-White glass", *The Connoisseur,* June—July 1966.
A contribution has been made to the history of Bohemian opaque glass by the so far unpublished thesis by H. Brožková, *Harrachovské mléčné sklo druhé poloviny 18. století* (Harrach Milk Glass of the Second Half of the 18th Century), Charles University, Prague 1978. Bohemian milk glass exported by the Harrach glassworks in Nový Svět is often considered as being a local product in the various countries where it is found. Besides these typical products with Rococo decoration, there also existed at the same time glass decorated with folk-style paintings in the Bor region.

Dutch Diamond-Engraved and Stippled Glass

Diamond-engraved goblet, Holland, 3rd quarter of 17th century

The engraving of glass with a diamond point, introduced as a decorative technique in the 16th century in Venice and in some glassworks north of the Alps working in the Venetian style, became in 17th-century Holland a matter for cultivated amateurs. Since the 16th century Berkemeyers in Holland had been decorated by engraving with a diamond point, and in the 17th century so were Römers, flutes, beakers and winged goblets or typical rounded bottles with tall necks. The earliest known Dutch maker of these engravings was Anna Roemers Visscher (1583—1651) of Amsterdam, who engraved on glass as occasion demanded Italian verses, calligraphic and flower motifs, fruit and insects after contemporary models. So did her sister, Maria Tesselschade Roemers Visscher (1594—1649), and Anna Maria van Schurman (1607—78) and in the last quarter of the 17th century another woman, Elisabeth Crama (Cramer).

The best-known of the amateur Dutch engravers was Willem Jacobsz van Heemskerk (1613—92), a linen merchant in Leyden, to whom a large number of bottles and Römers with calligraphic motifs are attributed. Another engraver known by name was Willem Mooleyser (mentioned 1685—97), whose most typical work are motifs of little branches and flowers with, in amongst them, figures of children and whole figured scenes. Peter Wolff (mentioned 1660—77) who lived in Cologne, was close to the Dutch engravers in his style. The technique of linear engraving with a diamond was also applied in the 18th century, when it was cultivated by Hendrik Scholting (mentioned 1763—64) and Canon Abraham Frederik van Schurman (1730—83) in Utrecht. An amateur glass engraver in Germany at the same time was the Hildesheim Canon August Otto Ernst von dem Busch (1704—79).

But in Holland in the meantime linear engraving gave way to a new technique, stippling. This spread thanks to Frans Greenwood (1680—1761), of English ancestry, who was born in Rotterdam and later moved to Dordrecht. This new method, with its uneven density of light dots, caused by the blow of a diamond or steel point, allowed the plastic modelling of a scene and became popular among Greenwood's circle. He was followed by the painter and graphic artist Aert Schouman (1710—92). Of the younger generation the painter David Wolff (1732—98) was especially productive. He decorated glass with motifs of putti with political slogans and portraits of important personages, including members of the House of Orange. His contemporary Jacobus van den Blijk (1736—1814) also copied pictures in the 1780s. The poor state of Dutch glassmaking in the second half of the 18th century can be seen from the fact that the engravers used almost exclusively contemporary English glass which, owing to its softness and glitter, was undoubtedly the most suitable material for the application of such decoration.

111/ Goblet,
diamond-stippled, with two
putti and the inscription DE
VRYHEYT ("Freedom"),
Holland (English glass),
Jacobus van den Blijk,
signed and dated 1777

112/ Goblet, diamond-stippled, with allegory of Painting, Holland (English glass), Jacobus van den Blijk, signed and dated 1777

113/ Goblet,
diamond-stippled, with two
putti and the inscription
HET WELVAREN VAN
THUYS DENAREN,
Holland (English glass),
David Wolff, around 1790

114/ Goblet,
diamond-stippled, with
three putti and the
inscription VRYHEYT EN
VADERLAND ("Freedom
at home"),
Holland (English glass),
David Wolff, around 1790

Advice to Collectors and Recommended Literature

Diamond engraved and stippled glass is very popular with collectors. It has been thoroughly dealt with by J. G. van Gelder, "Willem Jacobs van Heemskerk, Glasgraveur", *Oud Holland* LVII, 1940, pp. 181—191, F. Hudig, "De Glasgraveur W. Mooleyser", *Oud Holland* 43, 1926, pp. 221—227, "Diamond Engraving", in Wilfred Buckley, *European Glass,* London 1926, pp. XVI—XXXV and W. Buckley, *Frans Greenwood and his Engraved Glasses,* London 1930; *D. Wolff and the Glasses that He Engraved,* London 1935, then more lately by R. J. Charleston, "Dutch Decoration of English Glass", *Transaction of the Society of Glass Technology,* 1957, and H. Tait, "Wolff Glasses in an English Private Collection", *The Connoisseur,* June 1968.

Imitations of this type of glass are very rare, but it should not be forgotten that the production of diamond engraved glass still existed in the 19th century.

Cut Glass of the End of the 18th Century and the First Half of the 19th

Decanter with pipe, cut round the bottom,
Ireland, Belfast, beginning of 19th century

Decanter, diamond- and wedge-cut,
England, around 1820

The French Revolution was the beginning of social and ideological changes that were reflected in art and in public aesthetic opinion. In place of Baroque pomposity there appeared more "bourgeois" interiors and the accessories to accompany them, a rationality and sense of proportion corresponding to the sobriety of the Neo-classical and Empire styles.

Basically a classical element was the diamond cutting, with which English and Irish glass broke through to the world markets at the end of the 18th and 19th centuries. In England the cutting of glass came in around 1719, but only became widespread from about 1760. At first it was more like shallow facets covering a carafe or the stem of a goblet; later it was combined with V-shaped mitres. The spread of the technique of cutting on hollow glass was undoubtedly helped by the English production of cut candlesticks and chandeliers, where the facet cutting played a very important part.

In 1746 the English parliament put a tax on glass according to its weight and at the same time issued a ban on the export and import of glass to and from Ireland. When in 1780 the Irish won the battle for the right to free trade, they had a great advantage over the English glassmakers, who were subject to the tax. So at that time a number of glassworks grew up in Ireland, often financed with English capital and almost always operated by English glassmakers. The main production centres were the towns of Belfast, Cork, Dublin and Waterford.

Only then did the English and Irish glassworks begin fully to make use of the unique character of the soft and shining lead glass, and to develop their own style of cutting glass. Cut decoration, combining four-sided strawberry diamonds, wedge-shaped cuts and little printies, corresponded to the aesthetics of Neo-classicism and the Empire styles and to the taste of the customers. This glass was very well received, both in America and in Europe, and after the end of the Napoleonic Wars it became a model for French, German and Bohemian production of Empire and late Empire glass. Around 1820 flat stones began to be used, which were an element of inspiration especially for Bohemian glass.

At the end of the 18th century Bohemian glassmakers suffered a great market crisis: the decline of Bohemian glass, caused by their own out-moded forms the competition of the new type of Anglo-Irish cut glass and in addition the blockade of Europe during the Napoleonic Wars.

In the first quarter of the 19th century Bohemian cutters imitated the English

Beaker, pressed, with
sulphides,
France, around 1830

Bowl, engraved, with
strawberry diamonds,
England, 1720s

Neo-classical diamond cutting. But by combining this with their own cut decoration they soon found their own style. During the 1820s more complicated patterns were cut on Bohemian crystal. In the 1830s the Harrach glassworks in Nový Svět attained its peak in this field and became the most important glassworks in Bohemia. Simple diamond cutting was extended by a rich combination of flat strawberry diamonds, wedge cut fans and little stars and smooth convex motifs. The shapes of the glass had great fluidity combined with aesthetically balanced proportions.

In 1821 the Nový Svět glassworks began to produce glass ornamented with embedded incrustations of porcelain matter in French style, sometimes of enamel, the production of which continued till the middle of the 19th century. The "sulphides", as they were called, were obtained from the Paris firm of Desprez, founded by the sculptor Barthélemy Desprez (died 1819), originally a modeller in the porcelain works in Sèvres. Desprez made the sulphides, which were first embedded in glass medallions. Mostly they represented important historical and contemporary personages; some were cast after medals by Bernard Andrieu and others. Desprez sold the porcelain pastes not only to French glassworks but abroad too. After his death his son continued in the production until 1830.

At the same time as B. Desprez, P. H. Boudon de Saint-Amans was also making cameo-incrustations. However, the French production of glass ornamented with sulphides was soon overshadowed by English and Bohemian production.

The versatile Apsley Pellatt (of the firm of Pellatt & Green in London) had devoted himself to the production of cameo-incrustations in England since 1819. His glass of this type, most of ten small flagons, was of shining lead glass, emphasized with diamong cutting. In 1831 Pellatt had a special mould patented to facilitate the production of incrusted glass.

In Germany incrusted glass was made in the Brandenburg Zechlin glassworks, and portraits of outstanding Berlin personalities are most often to be found on their products as well.

Advice to Collectors and Recommended Literature

English and Irish cut glass has been documented by W. A. Thorpe, *A. History of English and Irish Glass,* 2 vols., London 1929; *English Glass,* London 1949, and W. Buckley, *Old English Glass,* London 1925. Of the later handbook on this subject we should mention W. B. Honey, *English Glass,* London 1946, and E. M. Elville, *English and Irish Glass 1750—1950,* London 1953. Irish glass has been dealt with recently by P. Warren, *Irish Glass,* London 1972.

English cut glass was sometimes copied by the north Bohemian cutters of the 20th century. It can be judged from the examples that have been preserved that the largest production of sulphides came from the Harrach glassworks in Nový Svět. The Harrach glass differs from the English cut glass with cameo-incrustations in the type of cutting and the use of glass with no lead content. The French glassworks often put sulphides into pressed glass. New information on the production of sulphides in Nový Svět is publihsed by J. Brožová, "Eingeglaste Pasten der Neuwelter Glashütte aus ersten Hälfte des 19. Jahrhunderts", *Annales* 1970, pp. 251—260 ff.

Transparent Enamel Painting on Glass of the First Half of the 19th Century

A charming interlude in the history of 19th century glass is formed by glass painted with transparent enamels. Its development is due mainly to Samuel Mohn (1762—1815) who, like his Baroque predecessors, was originally a porcelain painter. He started experimenting with painting glass in 1806, and one of his earliest works is a silhouette portrait, like those he painted on porcelain. In 1807 he opened a workshop in Leipzig, where he made glass with landscapes and allegories. In 1809 he moved to Dresden, and here we already know a number of his pupils and helpers, who include his son Gottlob Samuel, August and Wilhelm Viertel, Christian Siegmund, Carl von Scheidt and August Heinrich. His views, flowers and insects were most often painted on thin-walled beakers, cylindrical and everted at the top into a bell shape, with a border of oak leaves, vines, a spray of roses, etc., and all are full of the sentimentalism of the period.

Mohn's son Gottlob Samuel Mohn (1789—1825) studied under J. Schnorr von Carolsfeld in Leipzig, at the academy in Dresden and in Vienna, where he went in 1811. He evidently had a good knowledge of chemistry and the technology of paints. In Austria he made his living mainly by painting windows for castles and churches. But he left a number of views of Vienna and of castles and ruins in Austria on hollow glass, as well as genre scenes and allegories. He had a strong influence on a further important maker of transparent enamel paintings, Anton Kothgasser (1769—1831), originally a painter at the Viennese porcelain works, whose first attempts with glass evidently date to the time just after the Mohns' arrival in Vienna. As new research shows, Kothgasser was employed in the porcelain factory as "Dessinmaler, Buntmaler und Goldmaler", that is mainly as a painter of ornaments, who did not belong to the elite who executed figural painting, views and portraits. A number of painters from the porcelain factory took a share in the production of his workshop, which at first he only managed, being still under contract to the porcelain works until 1816; some of them were undoubtedly more important and better painters than Kothgasser himself. These were Franz Sartory, Andreas Peil, Leopold Lieb, Felix Frattiny, Georg Lamprecht and perhaps also a freelance painter Joseph Hawliczchek. The five notebooks Kothgasser left form an interesting document, as they include lists of goods put on the market or produced by his fellow workers. Since about 1815 the products of Kothgasser's workshop were sold in Nuremberg, or in the Viennese ornament shops, and they were available in the porcelain works. The workshop's output was very close to Viennese painting on porcelain in both subject and style. The painters used a type of glass called Ranftbecher with a thick cogwheel base and they only exceptionally painted on any other shape.

Even during Kothgasser's lifetime similar work was going on elsewhere, influenced by his workshop. Among works of average and sub-average quality there excel, for instance, portraits of the Emperor Franz I and Caroline Auguste, which came from the Egermann workshop at Bor around 1830. Glass with transparent chinoiserie is attributed to Carl von Scheidt. Franz Anton Siebel (1777—1842) and his daughter worked quite outside the Dresden and Viennese circles at Lichtenfels in Württemberg. The work of Johann Georg Bühler (1761—1823) of Urach is not connected with porcelain painting, but has a clearly romantic and historical character.

Townscapes and landscapes were also painted with opaque enamels, for instance in the Bor region and in Silesia. A special group is formed by glass with prints coloured with enamel; this includes Russian painted glass from the first half of the 19th century.

Advice to Collectors and Recommended Literature

After the publication of the history of Empire transparently painted glass by G. E. Pazaurek (*Gläser der Empire- und Biedermeierzeit,* Leipzig 1923; new edition 1976), there was for a long time no basic change of view on this production. But some further light on the problems of Empire style painting on glass was thrown by the recent discussion between R. von Strasser, *Die Einschreibebüchlein des Wiener Glas- und Porzellanmalers Anton Kothgasser (1769—1851),* Karlsruhe 1977, and W. Neuwirth, "Anmerkungen zur Kothgasser-Forschung", *Keramos* 1979, pp. 69—72 ff. It has become clear from new findings that a number of painters from the Viennese porcelain works took a share in the workshop's production, whose qualities equalled or even surpassed those of Kothgasser.

Copies and replicas of Kothgasser's glass are known from the production marked by Lobmeyr, and they were also made in the Bor region, possibly by F. Egermann's painting workshop, and later perhaps by the Goldberg firm in Bor: H. Ricke, *Glasprobleme, Kopie, Nachahmung, Fälschung,* Kunstmuseum, Düsseldorf 1979; Walter Spiegl, *Glas des Historismus,* Brunswick 1980.

Bohemian Coloured Glass of the Second Quarter of the 19th Century

At the turn of the 18th and 19th centuries glassmakers considered clear glass to be the ideal, but Romanticism brought with it a love of colour. Bohemian glassmakers were the first to grasp this trend. Coloured glass developed in Bohemia from the 1820s. The first colour tones, imitating precious stones, still showed a classical restraint in colour. The foundations of the production of Empire style opaque coloured glass were laid by Count Georg Buquoy; he invented black and red hyalith glass and began to make these around 1820. Hyalith glass was decorated with gold painting, imitating ancient decoration or chinoiserie motifs, most of which were painted in north Bohemia — at Okrouhlá, Falknov and Kamenický Šenov. This invention was soon copied by the Nový Svět glassworks. Friedrich Egermann (1777—1864) used glass from both these glassworks for the production of his marbled lithyalins. This invention of Egermann's was connected with his attempts to decorate glass with yellow and red staining which he succeeded in doing at the end of the 1820s. But the technology of lithyalins did not remain Egermann's secret. Soon it was being faithfully copied in the Nový Svět glassworks and the Nové Hrady glassworks belonging to Count Buquoy, which, however, in 1835—45 specialized in producing what were called agatines after the fashion of the period for soft pastel colours.

The later Empire range of colours also included gold ruby. The first experiments at producing this were made at the beginning of the 19th century, when Paul Meyr of the Vatětice (Kaltenbach) glassworks received a gold medal for rediscovering it. The Harrach glassworks at Nový Svět only started making ruby glass, decorated with cut strawberry diamonds in the 1820s. This was made with a mixture of lead. And only in 1840 did the Nový Svět works succeed in making gold ruby glass of Kunckel's type. The main fashion for colours, however, came in the 1830s. The glass was then coloured in the mass, by layering or by colour stains and lustres, and usual colours were cornflower-blue and emerald-green. In the 1840s green and greenish yellow glass came into fashion, coloured with uranium, and yellow glass, coloured with antimony or silver chloride. Still more often in the 1830s glass was coloured by layering, and sometimes there were several layers. Ruby glass, especially, coloured with copper, was used almost exclusively for overlaying clear glass. A cut decoration, that exposed the transparent layer underneath, gave the glass a richly decorative effect. Gold was used for colouring the pinkish rosaline glass that was made around the middle of the 19th century by both the Harrach glassworks and the Meyr glassworks in Adolfov. Egermann's yellow silver stain, often used even on glass painted with transparent lustre pigments, dates from the 1830s. A red stain, which was the exclusive property of Egermann up till 1840, was later in general use not only in the Bor region, but also in small glassworks all over Bohemia.

At the end of the 1830s Bohemia adopted from France the artistic fashion for pale pastel tones, which in glassmaking corresponded to alabaster and opaline glass, whether white or coloured to rose, pale blue and pale green tones. The glassworks in Nový Svět and those in south Bohemia became famous for their opaline glass. Rococo Revival paintings of flowers and ornaments could be applied excellently on layered and opaline glass. In the 1840s the Harrach glassworks in Nový Svět began to produce glass layered with white enamel, which allowed the use of enamel colours in a manner similar to porcelain. Quieter coloured tones were produced before the middle of the century by the Venetian-style technique of threading, which was introduced, together with the technique of "millefiori", at the end of the 1840s, almost simultaneously by the Josephinenhütte in Silesia, headed by Franz Pohl, and the Harrach glassworks in Nový Svět, headed by his uncle Johann Pohl.

Bohemian coloured glass achieved great success on both home and foreign markets and clearly influenced the production of the leading glassworks in France, England, Belgium and Germany. It is a testimony to the technological mastery of the Bohemian glassmakers. Bohemian glassworks made use of coloured effects well into the second half of the 19th century long after bright colour effects had gone out of fashion.

Advice to Collectors and Recommended Literature

Following G. E. Pazaurek's *Gläser der Empire- und Biedermeierzeit,* Leipzig 1923; new edition 1976, later literature mostly gives only partial new findings. The most important postwar contribution to literature in this field consists of the articles and studies by J. Brožová in the exhibition catalogues of the Decorative Arts Museum in Prague: *Bohemian Glass 1800—1860,* Prague 1978; *Bohemian Glass of the XIXth Century,* the Moravian Gallery in Brno, June —September 1979, and in partial studies, such as "Lithyalins and Friedrich Egermann", *Ars vitraria* 5, 1974, pp. 75—97, and *JGS* XXIII, Corning 1981, pp. 64—73. The production of the Bohemian glassworks was very extensive in the second quarter of the 19th century, and so Bohemian late Empire and Revived Rococo glass is abundant on the antiques market. However, Bohemian glassworks were still making replicas of Biedermeier glass at the end of the 19th century and in the 20th.

Bohemian Engraved Glass of the First Half of the 19th Century

The traditional techniques of engraving remained artistically in the forefront in Bohemia. Its temporary decline in the region of Česká Lípa at the beginning of the 19th century was the result of a severe marketing crisis. In the traditional refinery region of north Bohemia only naive mythological and allegorical scenes were engraved in the first quarter of the 19th century, celebrating loyalty, love and friendship, the ages of man, etc. According to the latest research it seems that the high standard of engraving was preserved in the first place by the engravers in Nový Svět, such as both Franz and Johann Pohl (1764—1834), who, like the Silesian engravers, engraved seals. Both Pohls are cited as teachers of the most famous engraver of the first half of the 19th century, Dominik Biemann (1800—57). Biemann left a wide range of signed works, in the first place excellent portraits on glass medallions and on Harrach beakers, which show his training in drawing at the Prague Academy of Painting. Biemann settled in Prague, but he seems still to have worked occasionally for the Harrach glassworks in Nový Svět. From 1825 he used to go to Františkovy Lázně (Franzensbad) for the season, where he made portraits of the spa visitors. His younger brother Vincenz (1811—48) was also a good glass engraver. Another north Bohemian glass engraver, Moritz Oppitz of Bor near Česká Lípa, also settled in Prague around 1840.

There were a number of excellent engravers working in the Kamenický Šenov and Bor regions in the second quarter of the 19th century. The circle of engravers from Mistrovice (Meistersdorf) includes the outstanding engraver Hieronymus Hackel (1784—1844), identified as the "Master of the Rising Sun", who worked in Celje in Styria (now Yugoslavia). One of the best engravers of the Pelikan family was F. A. Pelikan (died 1858) of Mistrovice, whose son and daughter were

[167

also both apprenticed as glass engravers. In his time Pelikan was as highly appreciated as D. Biemann. The slightly younger August Böhm (1812—90) also came from Mistrovice, and he later worked in England, in Stourbridge and London, in Hamburg and in America. His earlier works were influenced by Pelikan, whom, however, he surpassed in the mastery of large figured compositions.

Other north Bohemian engravers also sought a living abroad — in England and France, such as for instance Franz Eisert of Mistrovice and F. E. Kny of Oldřichov (Ullersdorf). The best-known engravers who worked in Kamenický Šenov include the Helzel family, Karl and Johann Günther and Karl Pfohl (1826—94), who served his apprenticeship with F. Egermann in Bor. He worked temporarily in Wiesbaden and in Paris from 1857 to 1864. He made use of the effects of engraving on layered glass. His technical virtuosity is especially evident in his so-called lithophanes — pictures engraved in layered glass. In the second half of the 19th century the best of the late engravers from Kamenický Šenov, such as Karl and Otto Pietsch or the members of the Knöchel family, joined the studios founded by the Viennese firm of J. & L. Lobmeyr.

In the region of the Jizera Mountains one of the earliest of the 19th-century engravers was Franz Anton Riedel (1780—1844), a member of an important glassmaking family that came to Jablonec from Falknov. The local engraving tradition lived on in the Benda family, later members of

(continued on page 185)

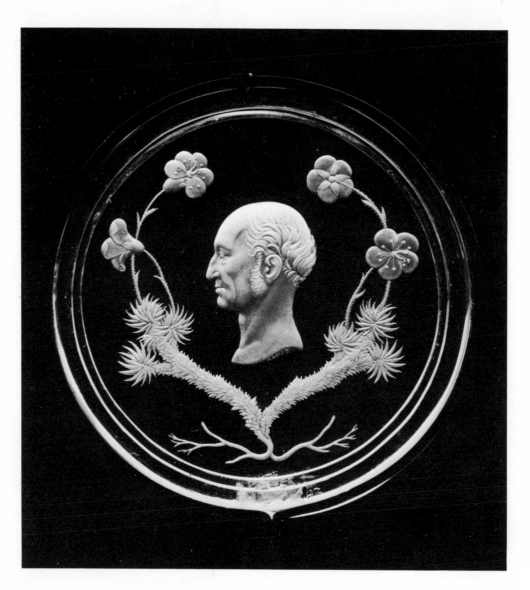

115/ Medallion, engraved, with a portrait of Count Kaspar Sternberg, Bohemia, Dominik Biemann, around 1830 (perhaps 1833)

116/ Glass with double-walled medallions: Covered goblet, engraved, with five double-walled medallions with silhouette portraits, Silesia, Warmbrunn, Johann Sigismund Menzel, around 1790.
Beaker with handle, brightly painted Madonna and Child in a double-walled medallion, Austria, Guttenbrunn, Johann Joseph Mildner, around 1790—1800

117/ Beakers with
transparent painting,
Dresden, Samuel Mohn,
around 1810:
Beaker with a view of
Rome.
Beaker with a view of
Dresden.
Beaker with a religious
allegory

118/ Beakers with
transparent painting,
Vienna, Anthon
Kothgasser's workshop,
around 1815—20:
Beaker with Aesculapius.
Beaker, gilded, with ancient
style scenes in the frieze.
Beaker with Cupid in the
Moon

119/ Beakers with
transparent painting,
Vienna, Anthon
Kothgasser's workshop,
around 1815—20:
Two beakers with
allegorical scenes

120/   Beakers
transparently painted with
portraits of Emperor
Franz I and the Empress
Caroline Augusta,
Bohemia, Polevsko
(Blottendorf), Friedrich
Egermann's workshop,
around 1830

121/ Beaker with transparently painted chinoiserie, glass probably Bohemian, painting attributed to Carl von Scheidt, around 1833

122/ Bohemian glass
imitating precious stones:
Lithyalin layered beaker.
Lithyalin marbled bottle
with stopper,
Bor, Friedrich Egermann,
around 1830.
Hyalith gold painted cup
and saucer.
Vase of oriental shape of
red hyalith.
Violet agate glass beaker,
South Bohemia, Buquoy
glassworks, Georgenthal
and Silberberg, around
1830—40

123/ Bohemian coloured
glass:
Cut beakers,
Bohemia, around 1830—50

124/ Uranium glass:
Covered beaker, vase and
sweetmeat dish,
Bohemia, Nový Svět, 1840s

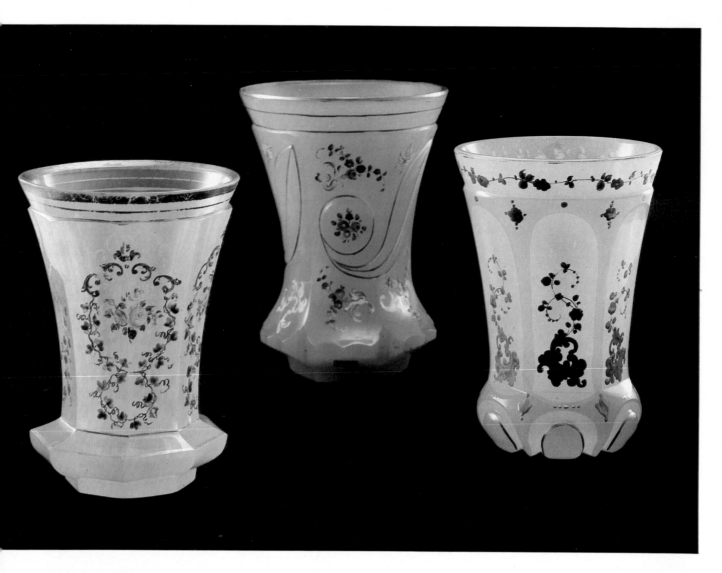

125/ Opal glass:
Beakers painted with silver, gold
and enamels,
Bohemia, around 1835—40

[178

126/ Bohemian blue
layered glass, cut and
engraved:
Beaker with bullrush motif.
Beaker with a portrait of
the Lord Lieutenant of
Croatia, Josip Jelačić.
Beaker with a deer in the
grass,
Nový Svět, portrait
probably engraved by Karl
Pfohl, around 1851/2

127/ Bohemian glass,
layered with copper ruby,
cut and engraved:
Covered goblet, with
a portrait of the Archduke
Stephen,
Karlovy Vary, Emanuel
Hoffmann, signed and
dated 1846.
Beaker with the Madonna
after Raphael,
Karlovy Vary, Anton
Heinrich Pfeiffer, around
1850

128/ Beaker and decanter, layered with rosalin and white enamel, brightly painted with enamels, Bohemia, Nový Svět, around 1850

129/ Revived Renaissance Venetian glass:
Ewer of marbled glass,
M. A. Testolini, before 1881.
Glasses decorated with aventurine:
A. Salviati, around 1867.
Seguso & Zanetti, around 1885

130/   Pseudo-historical glass, made for J. & L.
Lobmeyr:
Beaker with enamel painting in Islamic style, designed
by F. Schmoranz, made by Meyr's Neffe at Adolfov
in 1878.
Goblet of opal glass with embedded mica, made by
Meyr's Neffe before 1885

131/ Vase of topaz glass,
layered with enamel,
engraved,
England, Stourbridge,
Thomas Woodall, around
1890

132/ Beaker, engraved,
with a horseman,
Bohemia, Mistrovice, Franz
Anton Pelikan, around 1845

which worked there until the second half of the 19th century. Many reports have been kept about Anton Simm, who came from Kokonín (Kukan), one of the oldest glass engraving localities around Jablonec. His work includes many views, but also coats-of-arms, mottoes, allegories, genre and historical scenes. Beakers with the apostles are attributed to him, also with the silhouette of Napoleon, the ages of man, the Lord's Prayer and other things. But from the 1840s glass engraving ceased to pay: it was too expensive a technique for the owners of the glasshouses, and many glass engravers in Jablonec

[185

133/ Beaker, engraved, with a woman feeding Cupid in a landscape, northern Bohemia—Celje, Hieronymus Hackel, 1820—40

were obliged to take up other crafts.

Ever since the 18th century glass engravers settled in spa towns, where they engraved souvenir glass for the spa visitors. This applies to the west Bohemian spas of Karlovy Vary (Karlsbad) and Teplice too, where engravers from Mistrovice, Bor, Falknov and other places came during the spa season in the 19th century. The highest quality was achieved by engravers in Karlovy Vary, where engravers from the Teller family had settled in the 18th century. One of Andreas Teller's pupils was A. H. Mattoni (1779—1864) who had an engraver's shop in Karlovy Vary and employed a number of engravers. His pupil A. H. Pfeiffer (1801—66) also had a workshop, and in times of prosperity his employees numbered as many as twenty-five engravers. The last of the outstanding Karlovy Vary engravers was Emanuel Hoffmann (1819—78), an excellent engraver of figures and portraits.

Advice to Collectors and Recommended Literature

G. E Pazaurek's book *Die Gläser der Empire- und Biedermeierzeit* is still the basic handbook in the fields of 19th-century engraved glass. After the Second World War the work *Böhmische Glasgravuren* was written by S. Pešatová and published in Prague in 1968. New information is given in scientific catalogues by J. Brožová, *České sklo 1800–1860* (Czech Glass between 1800 and 1860),

Museum of Decorative Arts, Prague 1978, and by B. Klesse (with A. von Saldern), *500 Jahre Glaskunst Sammlung Biemann,* Zurich 1978. Monographs on Biemann have been published: J. Streit, O. Lauer, *Dominik Biemann. Lebensbericht und Meisterarbeiten des besten Porträtgraveurs,* Schwäbisch Gmünd 1958, and by S. Pešatová, "Dominik Biemann", *JGS* VII, 1965, pp. 83–106.

134/ Covered sugar bowl with diamond cutting, Bohemia, Nový Svět, around 1835

Mould-Blown and Mould-Pressed Glass

Glass blown into relief two- and three-piece moulds has been known since the 1st and 2nd centuries. This method allowed the cheap production of a large quantity of objects with relief decoration. Metal moulds with an inner relief were occasionally used by the Venetians and by glassworks worked in Venetian style in the Ne-therlands and elsewhere in the 16th and 17th centuries, in the first place mostly for shaping the relief decorated stems of goblets. The method was also known to Bernard Perrot in Orléans. Then some central European folk bottles for spirits of the 18th century were blown into their final form in relief moulds. In the 1830s large quanti-

135/ Covered sugar bowl of red opaque glass, pressed, France, Val-Saint-Lambert, around 1835—40

ties of this glass were being made, for instance, by Benedikt Vivat in Langerswald near Marburg in Styria, which he decorated with portraits of the Archduke Johann, Austrian coats-of-arms, agricultural emblems, and so on. But by that time glass blown into metal moulds was already being made elsewhere, including Bohemia.

The United States of America became the main world producer of mould-blown glass when they started around 1820 to imitate Anglo-Irish cut glass using this technique. During the second half of the 19th century glass blown into three-piece moulds exceeded all other kinds of glass in the USA. That is why the idea of pressing the whole vessel into relief moulds with a plunger, instead of by blowing, was developed into an industrial process in the USA. Pressed glass was first made by a workman named Enoch Robinson in 1827 at the New England Glass Company in East Cambridge, Boston, Massachusetts, and

136/ Vase of violet marbled glass, pressed, England, Sowerby's Ellison Glassworks, Gateshead, end of 1870s

137/ Bottle of lead glass, diamond-cut, with embedded sulphide, England, London, Apsley Pellatt, around 1820

later by Deming Jarves in the Boston & Sandwich Glass Company in Sandwich, whence the name "Sandwich glass" for pressed glass. Around 1830 Jarves introduced "lacy glass", which, with its decoration of relief ornaments of flowers and leaves on a background of small relief dots, broke away from mere imitation of cut glass. It was produced by a number of glassworks in the USA, and also caught on in France, where even earlier pressed ornamental stoppers for vials had been made and portrait busts, similarly to Birmingham in England and Nový Svĕt in Bohemia. The most important producers of pressed table glass in France were the Baccarat and St. Louis glassworks, whose glass was sold by the firm Launay Hautin in Paris, also Val-Saint-Lambert and the Zoude glassworks in Namur.

English glass forms a special chapter in the history of pressed glass. In 1831 Apsley Pellatt designed a machine for pressing glass there in the American way, though hand pressing had been widespread for some time before 1827. Most of the early pressed glass originated in the Midlands, in Birmingham it was produced by Rice Harris & Sons and by Bacchus & Green, and in Stourbridge by Richardson & Company. To start with English pressed glass mostly followed the models of cut glass, but in the second half of the 19th century it diverged from it. For instance, Sowerby's Ellison Glassworks in Gateshead often used opaque coloured or marbled glass, from which they pressed small vessels decorated with relief figured motifs in Victorian taste.

It is clearly evident in the case of pressed glass how glassworks copied one another in the 19th century. For instance, old French moulds were sold to various glassworks in Bohemia, where pressed glass was first made to any great extent in Nový Svět. The same thing happened with American moulds for mould-blown glass, so that at the end of the 19th century some Bohemian glassworks produced pieces of American glass of any earlier style for export to the USA.

During the last third of the century pressed glass spread generally. But with the practice of selling moulds and the imitation of commercially successful products of other glassworks, it is extremely difficult to decide the place of origin of individual products. The mould-blown technique using multi-piece moulds was also still used especially in making bottles.

Advice to Collectors

Whereas in the USA 19th-century pressed glass is highly valued by collectors, on the European antiques market it is rather a Cinderella, as its aesthetic values do not stand up to competition with the luxury products of the leading European glassworks. It is difficult to tell the place of origin of pressed glass, as the patterns and moulds were sold and imitated.

The Classical and Baroque Revival

Around the middle of the 19th century a reform movement rose in England that strove to raise the standard of design of industrial products, which had succumbed completely to the mechanization and commercialization of the over-rapidly developing industry. John Ruskin (1819—1900) tried to revive the artistic crafts on a religious and social basis. The architect and designer William Morris (1834—96), who became the leading personality of the reform movement in England, was active not only as the theoretician of the movement, but also as a creative designer. The "Arts and Crafts" movement in England, inspired by him, tried to revive individual craftsmen's skills at the expense of mechanized mass production. The eclecticism of the various "revivals" led to production in England acquiring a specific character and developing differently from the way it did on the continent, though in many ways it was a model for it. The cure for the evils of the time was to be a study and imitation of the examples of the past. In the 1860s classical Greek and Roman models had a powerful influence on English artists. In France during the Second Empire much work was done in a Neo-Pompeian style (Néo-Grec), and in England, especially in glass engraving, classical Greek ceramics were a model for form and decorative design. In this field glass-engravers who originally came from northern Bohemia excelled, such as J. H. B. Millar, who had settled in Edinburgh since the 1850s and who employed a number of Czech engravers. At Stourbridge F. E. Kny was an important personality from the 1860s, co-operating with the firm of Thomas Webb. From the end of the 1870s he undertook what was known as engraving in the style of rock crystal work, with the glass polished to a high sheen. Another glass engraver from Bohemia, who also excelled in this work, William Fritsche, also co-operated with T. Webb & Sons. The work of the English engravers, such as John Northwood, was completely different in character. He made his name with perfect classi-

cal engraved cameo glass, first on clear and later on coloured glass with an opaque white overlay. In the 1880s and 1890s John Northwood's son John II continued his father's work, and others in this field include the brothers Thomas and George Woodall, who gave relief cut decorations a more modern form influenced by Art Nouveau.

The revival of historical styles developed quite differently in central Europe. After the Revived Rococo style had faded out, Neo-Renaissance became the main style in graphic art for a long period. Its earliest propagator was Gottfried Semper. In the 1870s this style was widely accepted both in architecture and the furnishing of interiors and in the artistic crafts. Ludwig Lobmeyr (1829—1917) became the central personality in art glass at that time, co-operating with the progressive Viennese architects Hansen and Storck, and a number of other artists who designed for him decorations inspired by Italian Renaissance crystal and Bohemian Baroque glass. These designs, which linked delicate ornaments with figured elements, were then executed by the glassworks belonging to the Kralik brothers (Meyr's Neffe) at Adolfov in southern Bohemia, which made excellent metal, and also by engravers in the Kamenický Šenov region, where Lobmeyr founded his own refinery plant. Lobmeyr's style had a great influence on the whole production of north Bohemian engraved glass.

In Italy the classical revival followed the national tradition, then involved in efforts to revive the fame of the almost extinct tradition of Venetian glassmaking. Around 1859 Antonio Salviati founded a glassworks in Murano, based on English capital. After mastering the technique of mosaic, the company turned to making luxury historical glass in the Venetian style. It was followed by a number of other Italian firms, in the first place the Compagnia di Venezia e Murano, which also made copies of ancient glass.

The Renaissance Revival in central

Little basket with the handle and edge formed of a cane with an air spiral, called fancy glass, Scotland, Edinburgh, before 1867

138/   Plate, engraved, with putti,
engraved by Karl Pietsch in Kamenický Šenov for J. & L. Lobmeyr before 1878

Europe came somewhat later, at the end of the seventies, and looked for inspiration to the so-called "Old German" glass forms — Humpen, Römers, Kuttrolfs, Daumenglas, Spechter and a number of others. Factory decorated glass was made especially famous by the founding in 1879 of the Rheinische Glashütten AG in Ehrenfeld near Cologne, which besides Old German glass also made glass after Venetian and classical models.

In the 1880s historical Romanticism was in vogue, and glass was painted with motifs of armorial bearings, figures in historical costume and so on. There was a very large production of this type of glass. Besides the Fritz Heckert glassworks in Petersdorf (Piechowice) in Silesia, similar glass was made by a number of glassworks, including the Harrach glassworks in

Nový Svět and the Meyr's Neffe glassworks in Adolfov. Heckert and a number of others also made direct copies of historical glass.

The fashion of imitating oriental enamel paintings, which began in the 1870s, introduced a more elegant style. It was derived from Arabic, Persian and Indian models, and was used to a great extent, for instance in production for the Viennese firm of J. & L. Lobmeyr. Designs by contemporary Viennese artists and Franz Schmoranz of Prague were carried out by the Bohemian glassworks at Adolfov. In France Philipp-Joseph Brocard and J. P. Imberton worked in this style.

At the end of the 1870s, too, Europe discovered the art of the Far East — of Japan and China, which had an especially strong impact in France, where acquaintance with this art freed de-

[193

139/ Decanter,
diamond-cut crystal glass,
England, Stourbridge,
Thomas Webb & Sons,
around 1878

signers from dependence on historical forms and gave them a new feeling for flower and leaf decoration, studied from nature. The inspiration brought by this art was most successfully expressed in the work of Emile Gallé (1846—1904).

The influence of the Far East contributed to the development of so-called. "fancy glass", factory-made glass with applied and pincered plant decoration. In the 1880s it dominated part of English production, but was also made in France and in Bohemia. From Europe it then crossed to the USA, where it became extremely popular. Like other types of products that originated under the influence of the Far East, this style prepared the ground for the invasion of a new art form — Art Nouveau.

[194

140/ Ewer, engraved, with
ancient style scenes
(woman with cornucopia,
lion and putti),
Edinburgh, Josef Müller
of Oldřichov (Ullersdorf)
near Mistrovice, before
1867

*Advice to Collectors
and Recommended
Literature*

The decorative arts of the second half of
the 19th century have been rehabilitated in
the eyes of the public and collectors by
recent exhibitions and publications, such as
B. Mundt, "Historismus — Kunsthandwerk
und Industrie im Zeitalter der
Weltausstellungen", *Kataloge des
Kunstgewerbemuseums Berlin,* vol. VIII,
Staatliche Museen Preussischer
Kulturbesitz, Berlin 1973; A. Wesenberg,

W. Hennig, *Historismus und Historismen
um 1900,* Berlin-Köpenick 1977;
J. Brožová, *The Historical Revival —
Artistic Crafts 1860—1900,* the Decorative
Arts Museum, Prague 1975. The production
of the leading glassworks and studios in
England, France, Bohemia and Austria was
on a very high level at that time, even
though the average production is mostly in
bad taste.

For the history of glassmaking in Austria and Bohemia the handbook by R. Schmidt, *100 Jahre österreichischer Glaskunst,* Vienna 1925, is still useful, and deals with the J. & L. Lobmeyr production. English glass in this period has been dealt with by H. Wakefield, *Nineteenth Century British Glass,* London 1961. Recently this theme has been discussed in Walter Spiegl's *Glas des Historismus,* Brunswick 1980.

Art Nouveau (Jugendstil, Fin-de-Siècle, Liberty)

Around 1900 artists took their inspiration from a whole range of artistic styles, or mixtures of them. As in other branches of art, the development of European glassmaking before 1900 received its main impetus from France. The source of inspiration behind the new style in France was Japanese art, especially painting and ceramics. In 1878 the work of François Eugène Rousseau and Emile Gallé aroused interest. Rousseau (1827—91) was originally a designer and seller of faience in Paris. From the end of the 1860s he co-operated with the glassworks owned by the Appert brothers in Clichy. As a ceramics maker he appreciated the simple delicate shapes of Japanese pottery and the effects of running glazes, and he used these in his glass too. His vases were of transparent glass, with coloured layers, cut, decorated with engraved or painted oriental landscapes, chrysanthemum flowers, motifs of bamboo and peacock feathers. Other vessels were of ice glass with big coloured spots. Some of his works were a direct imitation of oriental work cut from jadeite. In 1885 Rousseau handed over his studio to his pupil and collaborator Ernest Baptiste Léveillé, who continued his work.

Rousseau was known only to a small circle of art experts, but Emile Gallé (1846—1904) of Nancy achieved amazing success. In the seventies Gallé and his father made glass of a historical character. The Japanese fashion only touched Gallé some time towards the end of the 1880s. With his sensitive feeling for nature, the Japanese-inspired elements grew into an independent graphic expression, which became Gallé's style, followed by his whole school in Nancy and by a number of others in France and abroad. Technologically Gallé's work from the end of the 1880s derived from Chinese layered and engraved glass of the second half of the 18th century. The decoration was not confined only to oriental flowers, but was often inspired by native flowers. From 1889 Gallé was appreciated and admired. His studio grew and produced more and more decorated glass, his pupils taking an active part as designers and decorators. Up till Gallé's death in 1904 this production was of a constant high standard, even though most of it lacks any personal touch. From 1904 to 1913 production continued in Nancy under Gallé's friend and collaborator Victor Prouvé.

Among Gallé's closest followers were the brothers Jean-Louis Auguste (1853—1909) and Jean-Antonin (1864—1930) Daum of Nancy, who made layered glass directly under Gallé's influence from 1889. Their output, which continued till the First World War, later became highly commercialized. Besides the French, Gallé's work had great influence on the important glassworks of the world, such as the Val-Saint-Lambert glassworks in Belgium, Kosta in Sweden and the Harrach glassworks in Nový Svět in Bohemia.

Towards the end of the 19th century

a number of small studios grew up in France making art glass. One of Gallé's contemporaries was the sculptor Henri Cros (1840–1907), who revived the ancient technique of shaping melted powdered glass in moulds, called pâte de verre. In 1892–1903 he made a number of large reliefs with this technique. The pâte de verre technique was also used by his son Jean, and by Albert Dammouse (1848–1926), Georges Despret (1862–1952), François Décorchemont (1880–1971) and Gabriel Argy-Rousseau (born 1885), who continued in this production until the 1930. Even though pâte de verre is nearer in its technique and final effect to ceramics than other glass products, it has its own typical poetic charm, consisting in its shades of colouring, partial transparency and sculpted effect.

In the USA Louis Comfort Tiffany (1848–1933) became as outstanding a personality as Emile Gallé in France: he was a cultivated and well travelled painter and designer. Tiffany's earliest work in glass was decorated windows, or rather mosaics of coloured glass. He drew great inspiration from his journey to the Paris Exhibition in 1889, where he saw Emile Gallé's work and where he was also inspired by ancient glass with an iridescent surface. In 1880 he patented a special type of iridescent glass, but he only started making it in 1893. In 1894 he patented the trade name Tiffany Favrile Glass for his products. In the 1890s he had successes at exhibitions in Chicago and in Paris, and he suddenly became famous not only in the USA, but also in Europe. Tiffany's designs made use of metal lustres and shining rainbow colours. Sometimes he was inspired by shapes from the Near or Far East, at other times by natural flower forms. Tiffany's glass, with its thin walls and decoration of embedded combed threads, is connected with Venetian and perhaps also with ancient tradition. The production of Tiffany's glass continued, unchanged in style, until 1924.

Tiffany's iridescent glass, which won a Grand Prix at the World Exhibition in Paris in 1900 (together with Gallé, the Daum brothers, Lobmeyr, Salviati

and Loetz-Witwe was imitated. The most important production of this type was the iridescent glass made by Johann Loetz-Witwe's glassworks in Klášterský Mlýn (Klostermühle) in western Bohemia, then the property of Max von Spaun. This glassworks, which made glass with Venetian-style decoration and embedded threads in the 1890s, was technologically well equipped for making glass in Tiffany's style. In 1856 L. V. Pantotsek was granted a patent for iridescent glass; he worked for the J. G. Zahn firm in Zlatno in Slovakia (then Upper Hungary.) At the World Exhibition in Vienna 1873 iridescent glass was exhibited by three firms: J. G. Zahn of Zlatno, Meyr's Neffe of Adolfov and E. Schmidt of Annathal. Three years later Lobmeyr also exhibited iridescent glass in Munich. The Loetz-Witwe firm showed iridescent glass at an exhibition in Vienna in 1890. Even the glass exhibited by this firm in 1893 at the World Exhibition in Chicago, with a decoration called Columbia, had a metallic sheen. But artistically Tiffany was undoubtedly superior.

Bohemian glassmaking was strongly stimulated by influences at home as well as from abroad in the period around 1900. Within the Austrian monarchy there was then close co-operation between the most important Bohemian glassworks and progressive Viennese artists, affiliated to the Viennese Industrial Arts School. Its professors Kolo Moser (1868–1919), Josef Hoffmann (1870–1949), later Michael Powolny (1871–1954) and Otto Prutscher (1880–1949) and their pupils, made designs either direct for the Bohemian glassworks, or through the medium of the above-mentioned trade firm J. & L. Lobmeyr or that of Bakalowitz & Söhne. Both these Viennese firms played an important cultural role in the history of glassmaking, especially at the turn of the century.

The Viennese Art Nouveau style has its own special character. It is cultivated, balanced and reserved in shape and colour, not rejecting the crystal tradition. It has a tendency to flat ornamentation. The Viennese ornamentation, propagated by the schools in Bor and Kamenický Šenov, imprinted its fea-

Goblet of clear glass with applied green ribs, England, James Powell & Sons, Whitefriars, London, 1895–1900

One of a set of goblets, designed by P. Behrens and made by the Rheinische Glashütten AG, Cologne–Ehrenfeld, 1901

tures for a long time on the painted and cut decorations of glass in central Europe.

In English glass examples of Art Nouveau are rare. We find them only in the work of Harry J. Powell (1853–1922), the main designer of James Powell & Sons of Whitefriars in London, and in the work of Christopher Dresser (1834–1904), whose designs were executed by the James Couper & Sons glassworks in Glasgow.

141/ Beakers of black-layered opal glass, made by the Johann Loetz-Witwe glassworks from a design by Josef Hoffmann, around 1910

Advice to Collectors and Recommended Literature

Glass products from around 1900 have for long attracted public attention. Detailed information on evaluating them can be gained from such books as W. Neuwirth's *Das Glas des Jugendstils, Sammlung des Österreichischen Museums für angewandte Kunst,* Vienna—Munich 1973, H. Hilschenz's *Glassammlung Hentrich. Jugendstil und 20er Jahre,* Kunstmuseum, Düsseldorf 1973, and the catalogue of the J. H. Bröhan collection in Berlin of 1976. Also A. Polak, *Modern Glass,* London 1962, gives an excellent view of glass from the end of the century.

The increased interest in Art Nouveau glass led to its being imitated. In America Tiffany, Loetz and other iridescent glass was copied. The products of various glassworks in the Bavarian Forest also have Art Nouveau shapes, or those of the firm of Schott in Zwiesel (with the etched signature AS). More recently K. Koepping's flowers have been imitated at-the-lamp (Karl Heinz Feldsbuch in Bremen). For further information see H. Ricke, *Glasprobleme, Kopie, Nachahmung, Fälschung,* Kunstmuseum, Düsseldorf 1979.

Glass between the Two World Wars

From the beginning of the 20th century a new independent aesthetic trend brought new creative principles to modern art, while the Art Nouveau style mainly applied to the decorative arts.

In France glass production evolved directly from Art Nouveau to Art Déco with the work of René Lalique (1860—1945), who had become known as a goldsmith at the 1900 exhibition. But at that time he was already experimenting with glass too. Luxury bottles, which he designed for the famous scent maker Coty, were still unambiguously Art Nouveau. In 1908 he founded a small glassworks at Combs, near Paris, where he made blown glass. In the glassworks in Wingen-sur-Moder which he acquired in 1918, he made decorative pressed glass. His earliest vessels are made of colourless ice glass with bright coloured spots; later he preferred opal glass. He used animal and plant motifs, systematically repeated. The majority of his work is pressed or mould-blown, but some pieces are made by the cire perdue process.

A completely different personality of modern French artistic glass was Maurice Marinot (1882—1960) of Troyes, a painter of the Fauves school, who became interested in glass in 1911. To start with he painted glass with enamels, but after 1922 he began to shape glass himself. He wrapped crushed oxides of metals on to a transparent core and then again added a layer of clear glass. His vessels were thick-walled, with simple profiles and a sculptural character. For shaping the surface he used deep etching. Marinot found several followers in France, such as Georges Desmoulin and André Thuret. The most important of them was the sculptor Henri Navarre.

In Austria even after the war the influence of the Wiener Werkstätte and the Viennese Industrial Arts School could still be felt, even in Bohemia. For a long time too the influence of the Viennese firm J. & L. Lobmeyr was strong there. This high-quality firm carried out the designs of Czechoslovak artists in the twenties, such as the figured vases by Jaroslav Horejc, exhibited in Paris in 1925.

Just as the Viennese influence began to decline in Bohemia, the independent style of Czech artists came to the fore: both the professors of the Prague Industrial Arts School and members of Artěl — Josef Drahoňovský, Jaroslav Horejc, Jaroslav Benda and J. H. Brunner, and also professors of the newly founded Specialized School in Železný Brod — Jaroslav Brychta and Alois Metelák.

The principles of functionalism, evident in the twenties in Bohemian and Viennese designs for table glass, began to take form as a point of view right from the beginning of the 20th century. In Vienna they were declared by Adolf Loos, in Munich by the German Werkbund (founded in 1907), where a number of architects from Art Nouveau circles met (for instance Peter Behrens, J. M. Olbrich, Josef Hoffmann). With the founding of the Bauhaus in Weimar in 1919 functionalism became the creed of a whole generation of German artists. Its main representative was a pupil of the Bauhaus, Wilhelm Wagenfeld (born 1900), who in the 1930s and 1940s designed simply shaped glass for the Württembergische Metallwarenfabrik in Geislingen and for glassworks in Jena and Lausitz.

Sweden was one of the strongest influences on modern glassmaking art after the First World War. This was thanks to the two painters Simon Gate (1883—1945) and Edward Hald (born 1883), who in 1916—17 started working as designers in the Orrefors glassworks. They softened the severe functionalism of the time with their sense of form and painted and cut decoration. Cased glass, called Graalglas, improved on Gallé's technique, and later glass called Ariel was decorated with embedded air bubbles. The engraved decoration on their glass was first influenced by the aesthetics of Art Déco, and later in the 1930s it achieved a monumental effect not only on the forms of glass in Denmark (Jacob E. Bang in Holmegaard), Norway (Sverre Peterson in Hadelands Glasverk) and Finland (Henry Ericsson, Artu Brummer and Gunel Nyman in Riihimäki), but also in Holland (A. D. Copier in Leerdam), England (Keith Murray), Bohemia (A. Metelák and Ludvika Smrčková) and the USA (Steuben Glass in Corning).

In Italy the creators of the new style were Paolo Venini (1895—1959) and Ercole Barovier (1889—1974). Venini founded a glass firm in 1921, together with Giacomo Cappellin and Vittorio Zecchin, that made glass inspired by Venetian Renaissance glass, and indeed directly copied it. Soon they started to experiment with the millefiori technique and threading, opaque bubbles and various kinds of surface treatment. The glass designed by Venini always had simple functional shapes, but colour played an important role. Another outstanding personality of Italian glassmaking was Ercole Barovier, who came from an old glassmaking family from Murano, and who experimented from the 1920s with colours and the surface texture of glass. Like Venini, he opened up new horizons for the modern art of glassmaking.

The period between the two world wars was immensely fruitful in the decorative arts — especially in glassmaking. The French feeling for ceramic sculpture, the strict discipline of German functionalism, the Scandinavian lyrical spirit and the Italian sense of bold colours and structures became important artistic legacies for today. Present-day glass designers can not only draw inspiration from them, but they must judge their present work beside this heritage.

Advice to Collectors and Recommended Literature

The most instructive publiaction on modern glass is still A. Polak's book, *Modern Glass,* London 1962. Another rich source of information for the first third of the 20th century is the catalogue of the Bröhan Berlin collection of 1976. The production of creative works between the two world wars was not very extensive, and so unique pieces of glass from the 1920s and 1930s are not found on the antiques market so far. But they do exist in the private collections of surviving contemporaries of their makers. From collecting art of the 1920s and 1930s it is only a short step to collecting contemporary studio works and designs by important contemporary artists.

142/ Vases, iridescent,
Favrile glass,
USA, New York, Louis
Comfort Tiffany, around
1900

144/ Vases, layered, etched
and cut,
France, Nancy, Emile Gallé,
around 1890

143/ Dark red vase,
layered, etched, cut and
engraved,
France, Nancy, Daum
Frères

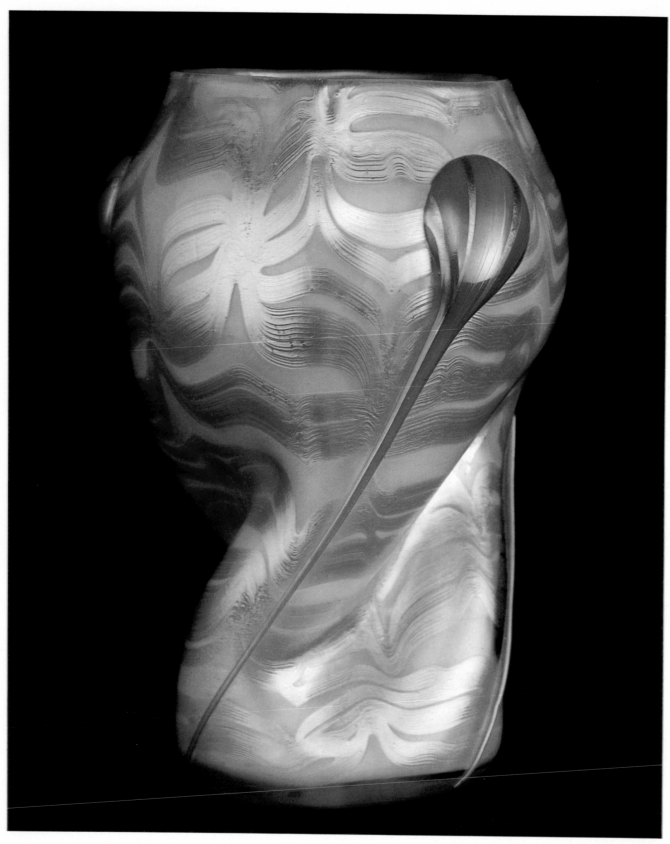

145/   Vase, iridescent, with
prunts,
Bohemia, Klášterský Mlýn,
Johann Loetz-Witwe,
before 1897

146/   Vase, furnace-made,
iridescent, from a design by
Marie Kirschner, Bohemia,
Klášterský Mlýn, Johann
Loetz-Witwe, around 1900

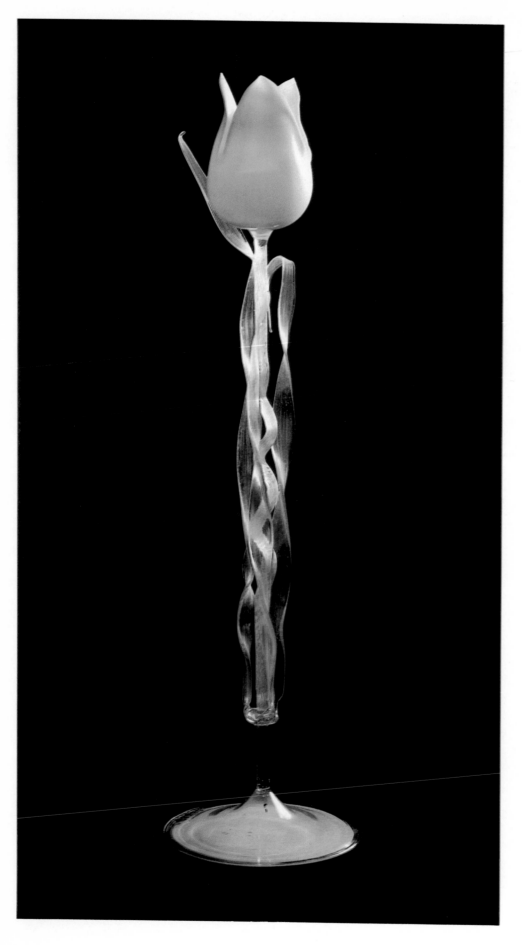

147/ Tumbler in the form of a tulip, blown at-the-lamp, Berlin—Wiesbaden, made from Karl Koepping's design by Friedrich Zitzmann, around 1900

148/ Vial of layered glass with pressed decorative stopper, Paris, René Lalique, first quarter of 20th century

149/   Vials decorated with
metal oxides, wrapped on
a molten core, France,
Troyes, Maurice Marinot,
around 1930

150/ Vases and vial,
furnace-made,
Sweden, Orrefors, Vicke
Lindstrand, 1930s

Covered bowl of muslin glass,
designed by Oswald Haerdtl
for J. & L. Lobmeyr, around
1925

Decanter and beaker,
from a table set,
engraved, designed by Adolf Loos for
J. & L. Lobmeyr, 1930

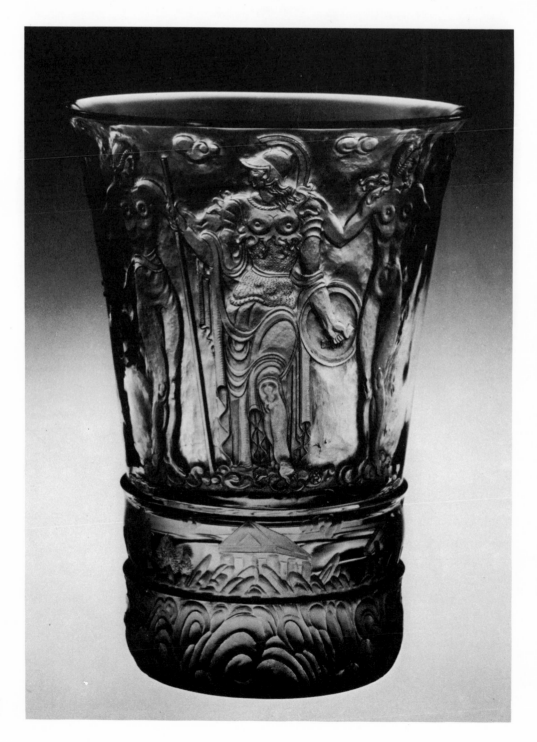

151/ Vase, relief
engraved, with three
goddesses,
made by Lobmeyr studio in
Kamenický Šenov from
a design by Jaroslav Horejc
in 1925

152/ Vase with silver
painted decoration,
Holland, Leerdam, Dirk
Copier, end of 1920s

Glossary of Specific Names of Vessels

alabastron (Greek)—a small cylindrical bottle for perfumes and scented oils, with a narrow neck and two small handles. In shape it resembles similar alabaster vessels (Near East, 600 B.C.—A.D. 100)

almorrata or **almorratxa** (Spanish)—a vessel with four spouts, used on ceremonial occasions for sprinkling rosewater (Catalonia, 16th—18th centuries)

amphoriskos (Greek)—a toilet phial in the shape of a small amphora (ancient Greek, c. 600 years B.C. — 1st century A.D.)

Angster—see **Kuttrolf**

aryballos (Greek)—a rounded toilet phial with one or two handles (ancient Greek and Roman, c. 600 years B.C.—1st century A.D.)

balsamarium (Latin)—see **unguentarium**

Berkemeyer (German)—an early variant of the Römer, a cup with a conical bowl on a cylindrical body (Rhineland and Netherlands, end of the 16th and beginning of the 17th centuries)

cántir or **cántaro** (Spanish)—drinking vessel with a rounded body, two spouts and a circular handle at the top (Catalonia, 17th and 18th centuries)

flute—a tall slender goblet for champagne (Netherlands, 17th century)

Humpen (German)—a large cylindrical beaker (16th—18th centuries, central Europe)

Igelglas (German) —a tall beaker, widening into a balustroid in the upper part (Germany, 16th—17th centuries)

Krautstrunk (German) — barrel-shaped beaker with everted lip and applied prunts, mostly of greenish glass (Germany, mainly Rhineland, second half of the 15th and first half of the 16th centuries)

Kuttrolf (German)—a bottle with a neck of several intertwined pipes (Germany, 15th—17th century, also Venetian-style glass 16th and 17th centuries)

Maigelein (German)—a small hemispherical cup of green Waldglas with a high pointed kick and optical rib decoration (Germany, 15th century)

oenochoë (Greek)—a ewer with an egg-shaped body and a tall handle (ancient Greek and Roman, 600 B.C.—1st century A.D.)

Passglas (German)—a large beaker horizontally divided by ribs into bands, indicating the amount the drinker should consume (Germany, 17th—18th centuries)

porró or **porrón** (Spanish)—a drinking vessel with a long spout for pouring wine direct into the drinker's mouth (Catalonia, 17th and 18th centuries)

Ranftbecher (German)—a conical beaker on a massive cogwheel base (Austria, 1815—1830)

Römer (German)—goblet for Rhine wine with a rounded or egg-shaped bowl and decoration on the hollow cylindrical foot (Netherlands, Germany and England, 17th—18th centuries)

Rüsselbecher (German)—a claw or trunk beaker of green glass, with two or three rows of hollow claws or trunks (probosces) and combs (Franconian glass, 5th—8th centuries)

Stangenglas (German)—a tall slender cylindrical beaker, like the English "yard-of-ale" (Germany, 16th—18th centuries)

tazza (Italian) — an ornamental cup — a flat or shallow bowl on a foot for fruit and sweetmeats (Venice, 16th—18th centuries)

unguentarium (Latin)—a small toilet phial of any shape (Pre-Roman, Roman and Islamic glass)

[212

vasa diatreta (Latin) — beakers decorated with a lightly attached openwork casing, cut into a regular network, with figural and other decorations (Roman and Rhineland glass, 4th — 5th centuries)

vasa murrhina (Latin) — luxury Roman glass objects made of mosaic glass, which imitated simpler vessels of fluorspar (probably Alexandria, c. 100 B.C. — A.D. 100)

Willkomm (German) — "welcome" beakers, used for greeting guests, mostly gigantic Humpen, but also vessels of different shapes, not only glass (Germany, 16th and 17th centuries)

Glossary of Technical Terms

agate glass (chalcedony glass)—marbled opaque glass with brown, blue, green and yellow spots, made around 1500 and again around 1700 in Venice. Red marbled glass was made in the 17th and 18th centuries in Bohemia (Siegellackrotes Glas). Chalcedony was imitated in the second half of the 19th century.

alabaster glass—see **milk glass** and **opal glass**

amalgam—alloy of mercury and another metal. It was used with gold for gilding glass, with tin for backing mirrors; in the 19th century for amalgamating double hollow glass and Christmas-tree decorations.

aventurine—glass with spots of oxydized copper scale (gold aventurine). It was used in Venice from the beginning of the 17th century, especially in the 18th and 19th centuries.

barilla (Salsola soda)—a seaweed that grows in the Mediterranean used to obtain soda by leaching. In Spain barilla refers to glasswort *(Saliconia herbacea).*

blowing—the shaping of glass with the aid of a glassblower's pipe, used from the 1st century B.C. Glass can be blown either freehand or into two-piece moulds, in which the bubble can be turned, or fixed into multi-piece moulds, in which the product gets a relief decoration.

bone glass—see **milk glass**

cast glass—vessels of cast glass were made by fusing powdered frit in moulds as early as the 8th century B.C. Cast flat glass (for glass panes and mirrors) was invented by the Romans, developed by Bernard Perrot in Orléans and perfected by Louis-Lucas de Nehou in 1688.

chalcedony glass—see **agate glass**

cobalt glass—blue glass (e.g. Bristol blue) coloured with cobalt oxide, known as zaffer. Cobalt is mainly found in Europe in the Saxon Ore Mountains. In Venice cobalt was used in glassmaking from the 15th century; at the end of the 16th and in the 17th centuries cobalt glass can also be found in England, the Netherlands, Bohemia and Saxony.

cold colours—lacquer colours or oil paint applied without firing. Used especially in the 16th and beginning of the 17th centuries in Venice and central Europe.

crizzling—a defect of a batch of glass shown by the glass losing its transparency, fine cracks and dampness appearing on the surface. It is caused by a lack of balance between the ingredients in the batch (mainly too much alkali).

crystal glass—clear glass of the best quality, similar to rock crystal. Venetian cristallo was made since the 14th century. The term crystal glass has been used for luxury clear glass not only in Italy, but in countries making glass à la façon de Venise, such as France and the Netherlands. In central Europe crystal glass is spoken of only in the last third of the 17th century. Bohemian and German potassium-lime crystal glass of the second half of the 17th century is hard, as distinct from Venetian cristallo, suitable for cutting and engraving. English crystal glass, made since the 1670s, has a high percentage of lead (24—30%), it is soft and shining and therefore suitable for cutting.

cut glass—glass decorated with patterns by means of rotating wheels of various materials, sizes and shapes. Flat surfaces (facets) are ground by using grinding powder (damp sand, emery) on large horizontally rotating wheels. Smaller wheels of various profiles, rotating vertically, are used for cutting patterns. The profiles of the wheels are flat or convex or wedge-shaped. Cutting is a technique taken over from the working of hard stones, used in ancient times (8th century B.C.). It was used especially in Roman times, on Islamic glass and in the 17th—20th centuries mainly in Bohemia, Germany and England.

diamond-point engraving—a decorative technique, making a linear drawing on the glass using a diamond or metal point. Used since the second quarter of the 16th century in Italy, England, the Tyrol, Bohemia and elsewhere. Owing to its simplicity, it was often used by amateurs, especially in Holland. In the second half of the 18th century stippling with a diamond point was developed in Holland.

double-walled glass—J. Kunckel described the production of double glass (**Zwischen-**

goldglas) in his *Ars Vitraria* in 1679. It caught on especially in Bohemia in the first half of the 18th century. Double glass is decorated with gold or silver leaf, in which the decoration is engraved with a metal point, sometimes supplemented with painting in transparent varnishes. The inner cup, so decorated, is protected by an outer glass casing, and the seam joining the two glasses is sealed over. When double glass was made in ancient times (fondi d'oro) the gold leaf was protected by a sheet of fused glass.

églomisé glass — flat glass decorated on the reverse side with unfired painting and gold or silver leaf.

enamel painting — enamel paints are oxides of metals mixed with glass frit, which has a good content of lead. By firing at low temperatures they fuse with the surface of the glass. They may be either opaque or transparent. Enamel painting was known in Roman times and in the Islamic period, in Egypt and Syria, from where in the 15th century it penetrated to Venice. In the 16th — 18th centuries it was used especially in Bohemia and Germany.

engraved glass — glass with representational decoration using techniques taken from processing precious stones:
a) **intaglio** — deep engraving, when decoration is formed on the glass by the engraver's rotating wheels (emery, diamond dust). The wheels, usually copper, of different sizes and profiles, are fixed to the shafts of the engraving machine, which from the 16th to the 19th centuries was a treadle one;
b) **relief** or **cameo** — relief engraving, when the background, not the design itself, is ground away. A water-driven machine was necessary for this type of engraving. The cutting and engraving of stones and glass were known in Egypt and Mesopotamia (seals and vessels). In Roman times it developed especially in Alexandria, Rome and the Rhineland. In the period between the 8th and 13th centuries this technique was used in Persia, in the 17th to 20th centuries it reached a high standard in Germany, Bohemia and elsewhere in Europe.

etching — the technique of decorating glass with hydrofluoric acid, which etches out places not protected by a resist (wax, varnish, oil). Etching has been common in Europe since the second half of the 19th century.

filigree glass (filigrana) — Venetian glass or glass à la façon de Venise, decorated with embedded threads of white or coloured opaque glass. The threads are either single — vetro a fili — or formed of plaited canes — vetro a retorti. Vetro a reticello or net glass is made by crossing the threads. Filigree glass was made in the 16th and 17th centuries in Venice and in glassworks under Venetian influence. It came in again around the middle of the 19th century.

fritting — the incomplete melted mixture of sand and alkaline ingredients which, after cooling, are ground to a powder and again melted in the crucible till a normal glass occurs. This is used for enamel paints and also when melting glass in the mould. In ancient times and in the Middle Ages, when the technique of melting was imperfect, pre-fritting was used.

gilded glass — this is done with gold leaf, gold dust or colloidal gold. Granular gilding also appears on Venetian glass and glass à la façon de Venise in the 16th century, when grains of gold dust were sprinkled on the molten glass. Gilding may be fired or unfired. In firing gold mixed with honey is used (dull gilding) or an amalgam of gold with mercury. Unfired gold is fixed on the glass by brushing with linseed oil.

glass furnace — the ancient Egyptians melted the glass in clay pots over an open fire. Since the middle of the 14th century B.C. we have known an improved furnace from Tell-el-Amarna, in which a temperature of about 1,000° C could be attained. The Romans had a **multi-chamber furnace,** in which the glass was also cooled. The **medieval furnace** was low, arched, semi-egg-shaped, built of stones and clay. Mostly it was taken down every six months and rebuilt, which is how glassworks were easily moved at that time. In Agricola's and Kunckel's illustrations there are always two furnaces — one for pre-melting, the other for melting the frit. Besides these there was a special cooling furnace, where the glass cooled slowly at low temperatures. The glass was melted in ceramic pots. Originally the furnaces were heated with wood, directly, without a grate. What is known as the Bohemian furnace differs from the old types in having a grate. Since the 16th century glass furnaces have been able to get up a temperature of around 1,500° C. In England, owing to a shortage of wood, heating with coal was introduced at the beginning of the 17th century.

glassmakers' tools: the **blow-pipe,** a hollow metal pipe about one and a half metres long, the **pontil,** a solid rod, on which the assistant takes off the partly made molten object from the pipe; **shears,** with a short head for trimming the molten glass; **long pincers;** a **wooden pallet** and **battledore** in the shape of a flat bat, with which the glassmaker forms the gather. For shaping the bowl of a glass, etc., the glassmaker uses **woods.**

Hyalith glass—opaque black glass made from 1817 by the Buquoy glassworks Silberberg and Georgenthal in southern Bohemia. Red hyalith follows opaque glass coloured sealing-wax red, made in the 18th century and earlier. Hyalith is mostly decorated with gold painting.

ice glass—crackled glass, the surface of which is cracked by plunging the hot bowl into cold water. In re-heating the fissures are slightly smoothed out.

incrusted glass—glassware with small fragments of glass fused to the surface. Used by the Romans (lst—4th centuries).

iridescence—iridescence on glass from archeological finds is of natural origin, caused by weathering. Artificial iridescence is caused either by lustre colours or by the vapours of the metal oxides on being slightly heated in the furnace. The second of these methods was mainly used in the Art Nouveau period.

layered glass (cased, overlaid, flashed)—is composed of two or more layers of different coloured glass and is produced either by blowing in coloured cells from other bubbles of different colours where the bowl has fallen in, or by gathering molten glass of a different colour on the bowl and overlaying with it. Casing was known in Roman times, and occurs rarely in Baroque times (Böttger's overlaid ruby glass). It developed mainly in the second quarter of the 19th century in Bohemia and, after Bohemian models, in England, France, Belgium, etc.

lead glass—glass with a large content of lead oxide (24—30%) which facilitates its melting and lowers the melting point. In Venice lead glass was used in making imitation jewels. In England lead glass vessels were introduced in about 1676 by G. Ravenscroft. Lead glass (English crystal) is soft, shiny, heavy and can be cut well.

Lithyalin glass—is opaque and marbled on the surface, a glass invented by Friedrich Egermann in Polevsko (Blottendorf) in

1828. The basis of it is mostly opaque red glass, stained on the surface.

lustres (lustre painting) — using metal pigments which, after being fired in a reducing atmosphere, produce an iridescent effect on the glass surface. Lustre painting was used in Islamic glass in the 9th—11th centuries. In Europe it was used in the second half of the 19th century.

milk glass—opaque white glass made with bone ash or tin oxide, sometimes antimony or zinc. Usually inspired by the attempt to imitate oriental and later European porcelain. It was made in Venice at the beginning of the 16th century. Later it became especially popular in the second half of the 18th century.

millefiori glass—originated by embedding cross-sections or brightly coloured canes of opaque glass into clear molten glass. This technique, known in Egypt in the 3rd—1st centuries B.C., was revived by the Venetians at the end of the 15th century. In the 19th century both ancient and Renaissance millefiori glass was imitated.

mosaic glass—millefiori mosaic made by fusing longitudinal slices of canes of different coloured glass, which then forms opaque striped ornaments and motifs. Mosaic glass of different coloured tesserae was used to decorate walls and furniture in Egypt.

opal glass—originates by opacifying the molten glass with calcined bones. It was popular in the second half of the 17th century (France, Italy, Germany) and the second quarter of the 19th century (France, Bohemia).

optical glass—(1) high quality lead glass for making lenses. (2) glass blown into relief moulds and then blown again, which softens the effect of the relief, so that the decoration is only evident to the eye as a darker shadow in the texture of the glass. Sometimes called optic blown glass.

pâte de verre—a mixture of powdered glass, a fluxing medium and metal oxides, melted in a mould. It is an ancient technique, revived in France in the second half of the 19th century.

potash glass—glass in which potassium was used as a fluxing agent. First it was made around the year 1000 in Europe north of the Alps. The potash was obtained from the ash of trees by leaching. Potash glass is hard and shiny, suitable for cutting and engraving.

pressed glass—is made with the semi-automatic aid of multi-piece metal moulds and plunger. It was introduced in the USA by Enoch Robinson (1827) and then perfected by Deming Jarves. Before 1827 this technique was used in England, and later in France and elsewhere in Europe.

ruby glass—red glass, coloured with copper, gold or selenium. Johann Kunckel developed the production of gold ruby, on the basis of earlier experience, before 1679, but this was soon imitated in southern Germany and Bohemia. The Harrach glassworks in Nový Svět in northern Bohemia made ruby glass with an admixture of lead from the 1820s. Only in the 1840s was gold ruby made in Bohemia, using Kunckel's methods. In the second quarter of the 19th century glass layered with copper ruby was also made in Nový Svět and other Bohemian glassworks. F. Carder made ruby glass using gold or selenium at the Steuben Glassworks in the 20th century.

Schwarzlot—a transparent enamel that was used in the Middle Ages in painting lines and shadows on stained glass windows. In the 17th and 18th centuries it was used by Hausmaler (freelance painters), such as J. Schaper and I. Preissler, on glass and porcelain.

soda glass—glass in which soda was used as the fluxing agent. It remains plastic longer than potash glass. All ancient glass was soda glass, as was Venetian and Venetian-style glass in the 16th and 17th centuries.

staining (yellow staining)—a mixture of annealed ochre with silver sulphide; it forms a yellow layer on the surface of the glass after being fired in the furnace. It has been known since the 14th century, when it was used especially on window glass; at the end of the 18th century it was used on porcelain and from the beginning of the 19th on glass (S. and G. S. Mohn and A. Kothgasser used silver chloride to produce a yellow stain in 1820, and F. Egermann succeeded in making a **red stain** in 1828 using the mixture of copper sulphide and ochre).

sulphides—in the last quarter of the 18th century in France and in the first half of the 19th century in England, Bohemia and Germany (Brandenburg) glass was decorated by embedded reliefs of porcelainous material. In England they were also called cameo incrustations or crystallo-ceramie. Sometimes metal incrustations and gilded and painted enamels are embedded too.

uranium glass — a yellowish-green and green glass, introduced in Bohemia by J. Riedel (Annagelb, Annagrün) around 1840.

Waldglas (lit. **forest glass**)—potassium glass of a more or less greenish colour, made by forest glassmakers in central and northern Europe from the Middle Ages to the 18th century. Its green colour is caused by the alloys of iron from the impure potash.

List of Illustrations

(Numbers in bold indicate
colour photographs)

Glass with manganese layered bowl.
Two-handled bowl of reticulated glass

20 Opal glass,
Venice, end of 17th century:
Ewer, cup and saucer

21 Chalcedony glass,
Venice, around 1700:
Bottle with silver mount.
Cup with two pincered handles.
Cup in the shape of a Greek kylix

22 Late Venetian enamel-painted glass,
Venice, perhaps the Brussa workshop,
1st half of 18th century:
Two bottles with Baroque flowers

23 Plate of milk glass, painted in sepia,
with a view of the Church of SS. Giovanni
e Paolo in Venice,
Venice, Miotti workshop (al Gesù),
1738—41.
The writer Horace Walpole brought this
set of plates from Venice to England in
1741.

24 Covered goblet, enamel-painted, with
the coats-of-arms of Hans Kleebichler and
Barbara Fieger of Hall,
Tyrol, Hall, around 1550

25 Tyrolean glass, diamond-engraved,
Tyrol, Hall or Innsbruck, around 1570—90:
Two goblets with motifs of the two-headed
eagle, clear and green.
Humpen with unknown coat-of-arms and
the inscription *Johann Sigmund von
Freysing*

26 Filigree glass from north of the Alps,
probably Bohemia, beginning of 17th
century:
Mug with pewter lid.
Humpen with bell-shaped foot

27 Glass from north of the Alps,
diamond-engraved and painted in unfired
colours,
Bohemia, lst quarter of 17th century:
Beaker with dancing couples, dated 1621.
Beaker with allegory Caritas and the
Žerotín coat-of-arms

28 Little vase, enamel-painted, with
leaves and birds,
Catalonia, Barcelona, end of 16th century

29 Two jugs, furnace decorated "nipt
diamond waies",
England, London, George Ravenscroft,
end of 1670s

30 Winged goblet with coat-of-arms,
diamond-engraved, called a verre à serpent,
southern Netherlands, 3rd quarter of 17th
century

31 Beaker of manganese glass with
pincered ribs and prunts,
Netherlands, Antwerp, 1st half of 17th
century

32 Beaker with white, red and blue
threads,
Netherlands, around 1600

33 Bottle with applied ribs,
diamond-engraved,
Netherlands, 3rd quarter of 17th century

34 Goblet with a plastic flower in the
stem, called a verre à fleur,
southern Netherlands, 2nd—3rd quarter of
17th century

35 Central European glass in the
Venetian style:
Winged goblet with lid decorated with an
eagle,
Bohemia, Austria or Germany, around
1650.
Covered goblet with a plastic flower in the
stem,
Bohemia, around 1680

36 Opal glass in the Venetian style:
Gadrooned goblet with ribs and applied
decorations,
France, 3rd quarter of 17th century.
Two-handled covered bowl decorated with
gadrooning,
France or Bohemia, around 1670—80

37 Ewer of yellowish glass with combed
white threads,
Catalonia, perhaps Barcelona, end of 16th
century

38 Cántir with optical and pincered
decoration,
Catalonia, 18th century

39 Southern Spanish glass:
Bottle with pincered free ribs,
Almería (María), 17th century.
Footed bowl,
Granada, 18th century

40 Furnace-made central European glass:
Beaker with pincered spiral rib and free
rings,
1st half of 17th century.
Beaker with pincered, spirally coiled,
applied trailing,
around the middle of 17th century

41   Joke goblet, optically ribbed, with the figure of a deer,
central Europe, around the middle of 17th century

42   Römers:
Small green Römer with a foot of drawn thread,
Germany, 1st half of 18th century.
Römer of clear glass with a foot of drawn thread and raspberry prunts, diamond, engraved decoration on the bowl,
Germany, end of 17th century

43   Yellow glass bottle for liqueurs, with optical decoration of lentils,
Tyrol or southern Germany, end of 17th century — beginning of 18th

44   Beaker, called a Daumenglas, of green glass,
Germany, around the middle of 17th century

45   South German enamel-painted glass:
Humpen with the coat-of-arms of Philippe Oyrll von Hertogenbusch, dated 1590.
Humpen with unknown coat-of-arms, southern Germany, 1570—90.
Venetian beaker with the coat-of-arms of the Helds from the 1st half of the 16th century, which was a model for these Humpen

46   Enamel-painted Humpen, with
The Adoration of the Three Kings,
Bohemia, dated 1578

47   Bohemian enamel-painted glass:
Glass with free rings and a hunting scene, dated 1594.
Jug of cobalt glass with a scene from an animal fable, dated 1592.
Jug with plant ornament, dated 1601

48   Enamel-painted Humpens of glassmaking families:
Humpen with a view of the glassworks in Zeilberg, dedicated to Caspar Steiner of Volpersdorf by the master of the glassworks Christian Preussler,
Silesia, dated 1680.
Humpen with a group portrait of the family of the master of the glassworks Martin Müller of Schmalenbuch,
Upper Franconia, dated 1654

49   Enamel-painted Saxon glass:
Jug with St. George, flowers and the inscription George Ferdinand Sieche, dated 1680.
Beaker with an equestrian portrait of Johann Georg III of Saxony, dated 1683.

Bottle with the allegories of Autumn and Fire, dated 1670

50   Enamel-painted Franconian glass:
Humpen with a view of Fichtelberg, dated 1669.
Humpen with the Last Supper, dated 1660

51   Goblet, enamel-painted, with parable of the Good Shepherd,
Bohemia or Silesia, dated 1767

52   Covered mug with the Madonna on the moon — Assunta and Schürer coat-of-arms,
Bohemia, dated 1647

53   Beaker, white threaded and enamel-painted, with the coat-of-arms of Johann Georg II of Saxony, wreathed in the Order of the Garter,
Saxony, dated 1678

54   Beaker painted in black and white enamel, showing the distilling of spirits,
Franconia or Bohemia, around 1670—80

55   Covered goblet, enamel-painted, with a landscape and strapwork,
Dresden, Johann Friedrich Meyer, around 1720—30

56   Panel, engraved, with a portrait of Christian II of Saxony,
Caspar Lehmann, Prague 1602, or Dresden 1606

57   Beaker, engraved, with the allegories of Potestas, Nobilitas, Liberalitas, after J. Sadeler, and the coats-of-arms of Wolf Sigmund of Losenstein and Susan of Rogendorf, Prague, Caspar Lehmann, signed and dated 1605

58   Bottle, engraved, with the coat-of-arms of Moritz von Sachsen-Zeitz, his monogram and that of his wife, Dorothea Maria von Sachsen-Weimar, Thuringia, dated 1655

59   Flute, engraved, with flower decoration and vases,
a German engraver working in the northern Netherlands, around 1660—70

60   Flute, engraved, with decoration of sunflowers and animals, Nuremberg, around 1670—80

61   Goblet, engraved, with Bacchus and putti,
a German engraver working in the northern Netherlands, around 1660—70

62   Goblet, engraved, with Athena and the lion,
Nuremberg, attributed to Hermann Schwinger, around 1670—80

63   Goblet, engraved, with a view of a battle,
Nuremberg, Johann Wolfgang Schmidt, about 1680

64   Goblet, engraved, with exotic birds in a landscape,
Bohemia, around 1670—80

65   Sweetmeat bowl, engraved, with flower and fruit motifs,
Bohemia, around 1680

66   Beaker, engraved, with grotesque ornament in the style of Jean Berain,
northern Bohemia, around 1720—30

67   Goblet, engraved, with a portrait of Charles VI after P. H. Müller's coronation medal of 1711,
northern Bohemia, around 1720

68   Covered goblet, engraved, with a portrait of Charles III (VI) as King of Spain,
northern Bohemia, 1705—11

69   Covered flute, cut with printies and wedges,
Bohemia, about 1720

70   Covered goblet, engraved in relief, with a plastic volute and the Schaffgotsch coat-of-arms,
Silesia, Petersdorf, Friedrich Winter, around 1700

71   Goblet with plastic volute and engraved flowers,
Silesia, Petersdorf, Friedrich Winter's workshop, 1710—20

72   Beaker, engraved in intaglio and relief, with putti on deer,
Silesia, Petersdorf, Friedrich Winter, around 1700

73   Beaker, engraved, with allegorical figures of the five senses after Martin de Vos,
Silesia, around 1680

74   Goblet, engraved, with small flower decoration and the coat-of-arms of Melchior Ducius von Wallenberg, castellan of Kynast,
Silesia (Bohemian glass, Silesian engraving), around 1715

75   Covered goblet, engraved, with a view of Wrocław (Breslau) and a portrait of Frederick of Prussia in a medaillion,
Silesia, around 1750

76   Beaker, engraved, with a garden scene and the Schaffgotsch motto *Aucun temps ne me change,*
Silesia, around 1720

77   Covered beaker, engraved, with a pastoral scene between an ornament of broad strapwork,
Silesia, Warmbrunn, attributed to Christian Gottfried Schneider, around 1730—40

78   Beaker, engraved, with the figure of a gentleman between Rococo ornaments,
Silesia, Warmbrunn, attributed to Christian Gottfried Schneider, around 1750

79   Beaker, engraved, with festoons of fruit,
Brandenburg, Potsdam, Martin Winter's and Gottfried Spiller's workshop, around 1680

80   Covered goblet, engraved, with Bacchus on a barrel and a townscape, inscription *Ehrlich leben und fröhlich sein* ("Live honest and be happy"),
Brandenburg, Potsdam, engraved in the style of Elias Rosbach, around 1725

81   Goblet, engraved, with a river god in a landscape, inscription *Des Landes Wohlfahrt* ("Welfare of the country"),
Brandenburg, Zechlin, Elias Rosbach, around 1740

82   Goblet, engraved, with putti and festoons,
Brandenburg, Zechlin, Elias Rosbach, signed and dated 1740

83   Four-sided bottle, engraved, with chinoiserie,
Nuremberg, Anton Wilhelm Mäuerl, around 1720

84   Covered goblet, engraved, with an allegorical figure of Justice,
Nuremberg, Anton Wilhelm Mäuerl, around 1720

85   Goblet, engraved, with the coat-of-arms of Friedrich II of Saxony-Gotha,
Thuringia, Georg Ernst Kunckel, around 1720

86   Goblet, engraved, with a hunting scene,

Thuringia, follower of Georg Ernst
Kunckel, around 1720—30

87   Beaker, engraved, with Diana and
Actaeon between rocaille ornaments,
Thuringia or Brunswick, Johann Heinrich
Balthasar Sang, around 1745

88   Flute, engraved, with hunting scenes in
medallions between strapwork and leaf
tendril ornament,
Saxony, Dresden, around 1720

89   Goblet, engraved, with Orpheus
among the animals,
Saxony, Dresden, around 1710—15

90   Covered goblet, engraved in relief,
with a portrait of Augustus the Strong,
Berlin or Dresden, around 1720

91   Goblet, engraved, with a bacchanal,
Saxony, Dresden, around 1720

92   Goblet, engraved, with a bust of Maria
Theresia and cross faceting,
Saxony, around 1745

93   Funnel-shaped goblet, engraved, with
a townscape,
Hessen, around 1750

94   Goblet, engraved, with a coat-of-arms,
Hessen or Lauenstein, around 1760—70

95   Goblet, engraved, with a portrait of
Charles XII of Sweden and a view of the
Battle of Narva,
Sweden, dated 1700

96   Goblet, engraved, with a bust of
Russian Czarina Jelizaveta Petrovna
(1745—62),
Russia, around 1750

97   Covered beaker painted in
Schwarzlot, with the bust of a man in
a medallion and landscape,
Nuremberg, Johann Schaper, dated 1666

98   Beaker painted in Schwarzlot with
a lion hunt, after A. Tempesta,
Nuremberg, monogramist H. G., dated
1673

99   Covered goblet painted in Schwarzlot.
with an allegory of Abundantia,
eastern Bohemia, Kunštát, Ignaz Preissler,
around 1730

100   Bowl painted in Schwarzlot with the
Kolowrat coat-of-arms and grotesque
ornament,

eastern Bohemia, Kunštát, Ignaz Preissler,
around 1725

101   Goblet, engraved, with allegorical
figures of War and Peace,
Nuremberg, attributed to Hermann
Schwinger, around 1670—80

102   Covered goblet, engraved, with
figures of the Emperor and the Turkish
Sultan on Horseback,
northern Bohemia, probably the Jablonec
region, around 1730

103   Ruby glass and ruby threaded glass,
cut faceting,
Bohemia, around 1690

104   Ruby glass, optically ribbed and
engraved, in gilded mounts,
southern Germany, around 1700

105   Beaker, double-walled, decorated
with engraved flowers in gold leaf and red
transparent varnish,
Bohemia, around 1710

106   Goblet, double-walled, decorated
with engraving of a riding school scene in
gold leaf,
Bohemia, around 1720—25

107   Detail of transparently painted
double-walled goblet,
Bohemia, around 1745

108   Mug of milk glass, enamel-painted,
with allegorical figure of Africa,
Bohemia, Nový Svět, around 1770

109   Cup and saucer of milk glass,
enamel-painted, with motifs from oriental
porcelain,
Thuringia, around 1745—50

110   Vase and inkwell of milk glass
painted with enamel,
northern Bohemia, Bor region, 3rd quarter
of 18th century

111   Goblet, diamond-stippled, with two
putti and the inscription DE VRYHEYT
("Freedom"),
Holland (English glass), Jacobus van den
Blijk, signed and dated 1777

112   Goblet, diamond-stippled, with
allegory of Painting,
Holland (English glass), Jacobus van den
Blijk, signed and dated 1777

113   Goblet, diamond-stippled, with two
putti and the inscription HET WELVAREN

VAN THUYS DENAREN,
Holland (English glass), David Wolff,
around 1790

114   Goblet, diamond-stippled, with three
putti and the inscription VRYHEYT IN
VADERLAND ("Freedom at home"),
Holland (English glass), David Wolff,
around 1790

115   Medallion, engraved, with a portrait
of Count Kašpar Šternberk,
Bohemia, Dominik Biemann, around 1830
(perhaps 1833)

116   Glass with double-walled medallions:
Covered goblet, engraved, with five
double-walled medallions with silhouette
portraits,
Silesia, Warmbrunn, Johann Sigismund
Menzel, around 1790.
Beaker with handle, brightly painted
Madonna and Child in a double-walled
medallion,
Austria, Guttenbrunn, Johann Joseph
Mildner, around 1790—1800

117   Beakers with transparent painting,
Dresden, Samuel Mohn, around 1810:
Beaker with a view of Rome.
Beaker with a view of Dresden.
Beaker with a religious allegory

118   Beakers with transparent painting,
Vienna, Anthon Kothgasser's workshop,
around 1815—20:
Beaker with Aesculapius.
Beaker, gilded, with ancient style scenes in
the frieze.
Beaker with Cupid on the Moon

119   Beakers with transparent painting,
Vienna, Anthon Kothgasser's workshop,
around 1815—20:
Two beakers with allegorical scenes

120   Beakers transparently painted with
portraits of Emperor Franz I and the
Empress Caroline,
Bohemia, Polevsko (Blottendorf), Friedrich
Egermann's workshop, around 1830

121   Beaker with transparently painted
chinoiserie,
glass probably Bohemian, painting
attributed to Carl von Scheidt, around 1833

122   Bohemian glass imitating precious
stones:
Lithyalin layered beaker.
Lithyalin marbled bottle with stopper,
Bor, Friedrich Egermann, around 1830.
Hyalith, gold painted cup and saucer.

Vase of oriental shape of red marble glass.
Violet agate glass beaker,
South Bohemia, Buquoy glassworks,
Georgenthal and Silberberg, 1830—40

123   Bohemian coloured glass:
Cut beakers,
Bohemia, around 1830—50

124   Uranium glass:
Covered beaker, vase and sweetmeat dish,
Bohemia, Nový Svět, 1840s

125   Opal glass:
Beakers painted with silver, gold
and enamels,
Bohemia, around 1835—40

126   Bohemian blue layered glass, cut and
engraved:
Beaker with bullrush motif.
Beaker with a portrait of the Lord
Lieutenant of Croatia, Joseph Jelačić.
Beaker with a deer in grass,
Nový Svět, portrait probably engraved by
Karl Pfohl, around 1851/2

127   Bohemian glass, layered with copper
ruby, cut and engraved:
Covered goblet, with a portrait of the
Archduke Stephen,
Karlovy Vary, Emanuel Hoffmann, signed
and dated 1846.
Beaker with the Madonna after Raphael,
Karlovy Vary, Anton Heinrich Pfeiffer,
around 1850

128   Beaker and decanter, layered with
rosalin and white enamel, brightly painted
with enamels,
Bohemia, Nový Svět, around 1850

129   Revived Renaissance Venetian glass:
Ewer of marbled glass,
M. A. Testolini, before 1881.
Glasses decorated with aventurine:
A. Salviati, around 1867.
Seguso & Zanetti, around 1885

130   Pseudo-historical glass, made for
J. & L. Lobmeyr:
Beaker with enamel painting in Islamic
style, designed by F. Schmoranz, made by
Meyr's Neffe at Adolfov in 1878
Goblet of opal glass with embedded mica,
made by Meyr's Neffe before 1885

131   Vase of topaz glass, layered with
enamel, engraved,
England, Stourbridge, Thomas Woodall,
around 1890

132   Beaker, engraved, with a horseman,

Bohemia, Mistrovice, Franz Anton Pelikan,
around 1845

133 Beaker, engraved, with a woman
feeding Cupid in a landscape,
northern Bohemia — Celje, Hieronymus
Hackel, 1820—40

134 Covered sugar bowl with diamond
cutting,
Bohemia, Nový Svět, around 1835

135 Covered sugar bowl of red opaque
glass, pressed,
France, Val St. Lambert, around 1835—40

136 Vase of violet marbled glass, pressed,
England, Sowerby's Ellison Glassworks,
Gateshead, end of 1870s

137 Bottle of lead glass, diamond-cut
with embedded sulphide,
England, London, Apsley Pellatt, around
1820

138 Plate, engraved, with putti,
engraved by Carl Pietsch in Kamenický
Šenov for J. & L. Lobmeyr before 1878

139 Decanter, diamond-cut crystal glass,
England, Stourbridge, Thomas Webb &
Sons, around 1878

140 Ewer, engraved, with ancient style
scenes (woman with cornucopia, lion and
putti),
Edinburgh, Joseph Müller of Oldřichov
(Ullersdorf) near Mistrovice, before 1867

141 Beakers of black-layered opal glass,
made by the Johann Loetz-Witwe
glassworks from design by Josef Hoffmann,
around 1910

142 Vases, iridescent, Favrile glass,
USA, New York, Louis Comfort Tiffany,
around 1900

143 Vase, layered, dark red, etched, cut
and engraved,
France, Nancy, Daum Frères

144 Vases, layered, etched and cut,
France, Nancy, Emile Gallé, around 1890

145 Vase, iridescent, with prunts,
Bohemia, Klášterský Mlýn, Johann
Loetz-Witwe, before 1897

146 Vase, furnace-made, iridescent, from
a design by Marie Kirschner,
Bohemia, Klášterský Mlýn, Johann
Loetz-Witwe, around 1900

147 Tumbler in the form of a tulip, blown
at-the-lamp,
Berlin — Wiesbaden, made from a design by
Karl Koepping by Friedrich Zitzmann,
around 1900

148 Vial of layered glass with pressed
decorative stopper,
Paris, René Lalique, first quarter of 20th
century

149 Vials decorated with metal oxides,
wrapped on a molten core,
Troyes, Maurice Marinot, around 1930

150 Vases and vial, furnace-made,
Sweden, Orrefors, Vicke Lindstrand, 1930s

151 Vase, relief engraved, with three
goddesses,
made by Lobmeyr studio in Kamenický
Šenov from a design by Jaroslav Horejc
in 1925

152 Vase with silver painted decoration,
Holland, Leerdam, Dirk Copier,
end of 1920s

List of Catalogues

Selected Catalogues of Collections

M. Bauer, *Europäisches und außereuropäisches Glas, C. und M. Pfoh-Stiflung, Museum für Kunsthandwerk, Frankfurt,* Frankfurt-am-Main 1975

S. Baumgärtner, *Edles altes Glas. Die Sammlung Heinrich Heine, Karlsruhe,* Karlsruhe 1971

S. Baumgärtner, *Gläser — Antike, Mittelalter, Neuere Zeit. Glaskatalog, Museum der Stadt Regensburg,* Karlsruhe 1977

A.-M. Berryer, *La Verrerie ancienne aux Musées Royaux d'Arts et d'Histoire,* Brussels 1957

E. Billeter, *Glas. Sammlungskatalog 4 des Kunstgewerbemuseums der Stadt Zürich,* Zurich 1969

B. Bucher, *Die Glassammlung des K. K. Österreichischen Museums,* Vienna 1888

R. J. Charleston, M. Marcheix, M. Archer, *The James A. de Rothschild Collection at Waddesdon Manor. Glass and Enamels,* London 1977

E. Heinemeyer, *Glas. Kataloge des Kunstmuseums,* vol. I, Düsseldorf 1960

B. Jansen, *Catalogus van noord-en-zuiderlands glas. Gemeentemuseum Den Haag,* The Hague 1962

B. Jantzten, *Deutsches Glas aus fünf Jahrhunderten,* Düsseldorf 1960

B. Klesse, *Glas. Kataloge des Kunstgewerbemuseums Köln,* vol. I, Cologne 1963; 2nd edition 1973 (with G. Reineking — von Bock)

B. Klesse, *Glassammlung Helfried Krug,* vol. I, Munich 1965; vol. II, Bonn 1973

B. Klesse, A. v. Saldern, *500 Jahre Glaskunst, Sammlung Biemann,* Rastatt 1979

C. Mosel, *Die Glas-Sammlung, Bildkataloge des Kestner-Museums, Hannover,* Hanover 1957; 2nd edition, Hanover 1979

A. Nesbitt, *Catalogue of the Collection of Glass Formed by Felix Slade, Esq., F. S. A.,* London 1871

A. Ohm, *Europäisches und außereuropäisches Glas, Museum für Kunsthandwerk, Frankfurt-am-Main,* Frankfurt-am-Main 1973

E. G. Pazaurek, *Die Gläsersammlung des Nordböhmischen Gewerbemuseums in Reichenberg,* Leipzig 1902

R. Rückert, *Die Glassammlung des Bayerischen Nationalmuseums, München,* Munich 1981

R. Schmidt, *Europäisches Glas. Die Sammlung Wilfred Buckley,* Berlin 1927

R. Schmidt, *Die Gläser der Sammlung Mühsam,* vol. I, Berlin 1914; vol. II, Berlin 1926

Selected Catalogues of Exhibitions not mentioned in the *Recommended Literature*

Ars vitraria — *3000 Jahre Glas. Ausstellung des Kunstgewerbemuseums Schloß Köpenick.* Berlin 1965

R. Barovier-Mentasti, A. Dorigato, A. Gasparetto, *Mille anni del arte di vetro a Venezia,* Venice 1982

Masterpieces of Bohemian Glass, Corning, New York 1981

Masterpieces of Glass, The British Museum, London 1968

Meisterwerke der Glaskunst aus internationalem Privatbesitz, Düsseldorf 1968

Sechs Sammler stellen aus Museum für Kunst und Gewerbe, Hamburg 1961

H. Tait, *The Golden Age of Venetian Glass,* London 1979

Trois millénaires d'art verrier à travers les collections publiques et privées de Belgique, Musée Curtius, Liège 1958

Le verre à travers les siècles. Musées des arts décoratifs, Lausanne 1972

Abbreviations

JGS *Journal of Glass Studies* (published by Corning Museum of Glass, Corning, N. Y., since 1958)

Annales *Annales du 1er ... 7ème Congrès de l'Association internationale pour l'Histoire du Verre* (Theses from congresses which were held in Brussels, 1958, Amsterdam, 1961, Beirut, 1964, Ravenna—Venice, 1967, Prague, 1970, Cologne, 1973, and London—Liverpool, 1979; published in Liège)

Index

(Numbers in italics indicate pages. Numbers in brackets are those of the illustrations.)